Finding Your Funding Model:
A Practical Approach to Nonprofit Sustainability

By Peter Kim, Gail Perreault, and William Foster

Contents

Introduction

Having a great program wasn't enough to achieve our mission, especially with all of the uncertainty in the economy. We weren't being very strategic about raising funds, which was leading to a good deal of angst and ambiguity about what we could realistically commit to accomplishing. We needed a funding model that could provide a level of stability and produce the revenue required to grow and deliver our programs at scale. Now that we have developed, tested, and refined our funding model, we are growing more than ever before—even while the recession lingers on.
— Dr. Tiffany Cooper Gueye, CEO of BELL (Building Educated Leaders for Life)

It's a paradox. Most nonprofit leaders spend an enormous amount of time on fundraising, but typically they have little idea how they will secure the money they need over the next five years. Their vision for how the organization's programs will evolve over that time, however, is usually sharp and clear. The rub is that a well-thought-out approach to raising revenue is essential to sustaining those programs and increasing their impact.

When they're small, nonprofit organizations often can meet their budgets by inspiring a handful of donors, seizing unanticipated funding opportunities, or cobbling together a mixed bag of funding sources. Charismatic leaders are often the key to swaying prospective funders. But as nonprofits get bigger, personal relationships and catch-as-catch-can are rarely enough to sustain larger-scale fundraising needs.

What's required is a *funding model*, which we define as a methodical and institutionalized approach to building a reliable revenue base that will support an organization's core programs and services. As Dr. Tiffany Cooper Gueye describes above, adopting and organizing around one such funding model put $17-million BELL (Building Educated Leaders for Life) on the path to financial sustainability and growth.

A funding model has three defining characteristics:
1. **Type of funding**: The model typically revolves around a single type of funding, such as government or individual, which constitutes the majority of the organization's revenue and which the organization invests disproportionately in developing. Other smaller sources often play complementary supporting roles but are not the focus of investment.
2. **Funding decision makers**: Within that principal source of funding, the model focuses on a particular set of people who dictate the flow of funds—

perhaps government administrators or a few wealthy individuals.

3. **Funder motivation**: A funding model takes advantage of the natural matches that exist between funder motivations and a nonprofit's mission and beneficiaries. These motivations range from altruism to collective interest to self-interest.

For BELL's funding model, the primary type of funding was government—specifically Title I funding through the No Child Left Behind Act (NCLB). The funding decision makers BELL targeted were the administrators of Title I funding; for example, for the Supplemental Educational Services (SES) provision of NCLB, BELL first reached out to principals, to secure access to their schools, and then to parents, to enroll students. BELL appealed to the motivations of those decision makers by operating effective programs that satisfied the SES criteria, delivering strong results for principals, and meeting the needs of families, thereby allowing the organization to tap this renewable funding source.

Underlying principles of nonprofit funding

This guide builds on two previous publications by The Bridgespan Group. The first was **"How Nonprofits Get Really Big"** (*Stanford Social Innovation Review*, Spring 2007), which was based on our research of nonprofits that had been founded since 1970 and reached $50 million in annual revenue by 2004. Only 144 nonprofits (excluding hospitals and universities) made the cut, reflecting the steep challenge of raising funds on a large scale. How those 144 did this defied conventional wisdom: The vast majority grew big not by diversifying their funding sources but by raising most of their money from a single type of funding (such as corporate or government) that was a natural match for their mission. Moreover, they created professional organizations tailored to the needs of that type of funding.

We followed up that article with **"Ten Nonprofit Funding Models"** (*Stanford Social Innovation Review*, Spring 2009), which catalogued distinct types of funding strategies that exist among large nonprofits. We identified 10 nonprofit funding models—defined by their main type(s) of funding, funding decision makers, and funder motivations—further confirming that the paths to growth are not idiosyncratic but strategic. (Please see "Ten Nonprofit Funding Models" on page 59.)

To help you and your organization navigate the process of building a funding model, we have developed this tactical guide. In it, we walk you through six steps (as illustrated in Figure 1 on page 3) for identifying and developing the right funding model for your organization.

The six steps take you on journey that includes developing an in-depth understanding of your organization's current funding strengths and weaknesses, identifying a variety of funding model options, vetting those options until you're down to the most viable one or two, and then developing a plan for implementing them. In Step 1, you'll **analyze your organization's current approach to funding**: assessing the reliability of your existing sources of funds, crystallizing why current funders support your efforts, and evaluating your fundraising capabilities. This diagnostic will help you identify strengths a future funding model could build on as well as weaknesses that may put certain funding models out of reach or signal the need for specific investments. This knowledge will help you home in on funding approaches that may be a good fit for your organization going forward.

Figure 1

Six steps

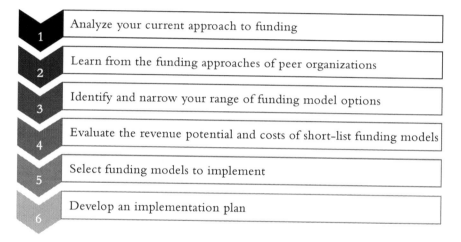

1. Analyze your current approach to funding
2. Learn from the funding approaches of peer organizations
3. Identify and narrow your range of funding model options
4. Evaluate the revenue potential and costs of short-list funding models
5. Select funding models to implement
6. Develop an implementation plan

In Step 2, you'll **learn from the funding approaches of peer organizations**, surfacing ideas you may want to investigate for your own organization. You'll also explore how any differences between peer organizations and your own might affect the relevance of their approaches.

You'll further vet these peer approaches in Step 3, when you **identify and narrow your range of funding model options**. You'll be screening for peer funding approaches that are both sustainable and replicable, and thus rise to the level of a funding model. In addition, you'll make an initial assessment of how feasible these models are for your organization, with the goal of selecting the two to four most applicable models.

Evaluating the revenue potential and costs of those short-list funding models will be your focus in Step 4. You'll develop an understanding of the funding available for each model and how much of that funding your organization could reasonably expect to secure given the competitive environment and your organization's relative strengths and weaknesses. You'll also estimate the investments (e.g., expanding into new program areas, adding staff, upgrading IT systems) your organization would need to make. This knowledge will put you in a good position to make an informed decision about which funding model(s) to pursue.

Step 5 is all about making that big decision—**selecting funding models to implement.** You'll draw on all you've learned in Steps 1 through 4 and commit to pursuing one or two of the models on your short list. Then in Step 6 you'll **develop an implementation plan** that will make your funding model plans actionable. The plan will describe in detail the investments your organization will need to make. It will also lay out a timeline for making those investments and implementing your funding model—assigning accountability to appropriate team members and specifying milestones and a learning agenda that will make it easier to gauge progress and correct your course as necessary.

Why bother?

Completing this six-step process will require a considerable investment of time and attention—from you, your colleagues, and your board. And you're unlikely to see a sudden influx of dollars when you complete Step 6. Funding models aren't opportunities to get rich quick. They generally require considerable time and investment to take hold. It took BELL four years of concerted effort to cover 70 percent of its site costs with government funds. There's also no guarantee that even the best-fit model will meet the nonprofit's funding aspirations. Why, then, do we advise many organizations to invest in developing a funding model?

Simply put, we believe that having clarity about how a nonprofit will fund its mission is as important as having clarity about how it will deliver its programmatic impact. Almost every nonprofit has two jobs, each with its own set of external stakeholders. One job is to identify beneficiaries and make a difference for them with programs. But beneficiaries rarely pay the tab—or at least not all of it. Hence the second job: cultivating a distinct set of funders. Building and scaling sustainable financial support is as complicated and important as figuring out the programmatic dimensions.

Identifying and developing a funding model is a long-term investment that requires patience, but we believe (and think soon you will, too) it's an investment that's well worth making. Instead of seeing every funding lead as a good lead, you can methodically assess each opportunity. Instead of wondering where and how to invest in development capabilities (and generally investing too little into too many), you can have an intentional approach upon which to build.

Is your organization ready?

At this point, you may be saying to yourself, "A funding model equals more money. Perfect! That's just what we need!" Well, maybe—but maybe not. Many nonprofits just aren't ready to develop a funding model. Here are some specific questions to help you assess if yours is ready:

- *Is your organization free of immediate financial distress?* You need to be able to focus on developing a long-term funding strategy. If you're finding yourself consumed by efforts to keep the doors open, chances are the time isn't right. In contrast, if your organization is humming along relatively steadily, but you just can't see a way to the next level of growth—now may just be the time to find your funding model.

- *Does your organization have annual revenues of at least $3 million?* We generally consider that mark to be the threshold for developing a funding model. As we indicated at the outset of this guide, nonprofits below that threshold—particularly those without significant growth ambitions—often can get by with idiosyncratic fundraising methods. There's no need to get overly strategic until doing so is necessary. (See the sidebar, "What about smaller organizations?" on page 6)

- *Does your organization have clear programmatic goals?* If not, you may not be ready to start this process, since strong funding models complement an organization's program model. They take advantage of natural matches between various funding sources and specific types of programs, services, or beneficiaries. Without program clarity, narrowing your search for the right funding model would be exceedingly difficult.

- *Is your organization willing to make the investments—in staff, IT systems, and other areas—required to fully implement the funding model you select?* We would only advise this process for organizations that are ready to commit to implementing a funding model. Otherwise, this process is bound to feel like a fruitless hypothetical research project.

If you answered "yes" to the four questions above, and you're leading a nonprofit with a funding approach that can't keep up with its programmatic ambitions—be it a $5-million organization that's contemplating developing its first funding model or a $20-million nonprofit that's seeking a new one—read on. By investing time and energy in reading this guide and thinking through its implications for your organization, you'll be taking an important step in elevating your organization's funding strategy to the level of importance it rightly deserves. We truly hope the experience helps you to identify and develop a funding model that supports your aspirations for making a positive difference in the world.

What about smaller organizations?

Even though pursuing a funding model typically isn't warranted until an organization reaches at least $3 million in annual revenues, some of the associated concepts can provide helpful guidance to nonprofits below this size. Practices likely to pay off include: focusing on types of funding that are natural matches for the nonprofit's work, clarifying who the main decision makers are behind those types of funding, and then understanding why those decision makers choose to support the organizations they do. And despite the natural temptation to cover all the bases by pursuing a wide variety of funding types, even at a smaller scale identifying the most promising ones and investing in them fully is critically important. Sprinkling development efforts across several is a recipe for under-investing in them all—and then not really knowing what could have panned out. Keeping these practices in mind will make it easier to develop a funding model if and when the time is right.

Considering a small set of options that could enhance a smaller organization's development work is also helpful, so it is not overly reliant on one individual's personal relationships or capabilities. Examples include hiring a chief operating officer to free up more of the chief executive officer's (CEO) time for fundraising activities, bringing in a new development staff member to support the CEO's outreach efforts, or cultivating or enhancing a fundraising board.

Getting started

Before embarking on this process, you'll want to spend some time setting yourself up for success. This preparatory work consists of clearly defining what success will look like and how you'll organize your resources to deliver on that goal. Considering both of these facets before plunging headfirst into the process will provide invaluable guardrails as you march ahead.

Clarify your goals

What do you want to achieve with your organization's funding model? Becoming more financially secure while remaining at roughly the same scale? Propelling rapid growth? Expanding into a new program area? This knowledge will help you focus on the options that will best support your ambitions.

Start by developing a clear and focused list of your organization's goals. An existing strategic plan may serve as a helpful starting point here. Consider your growth, programmatic, and financial ambitions.

Tips for getting started

- **Engage key stakeholders early and often.** Include your board, staff, and current funders. If a given individual could put your funding model plans on hold by making objections in the future, you should cultivate his or her buy-in throughout.
- **Be realistic about programmatic goals.** Recognize that you cannot do it all (as much as you might want to). Though your organization might want to expand to 10 new cities and double in size in your current sites, you may have to choose between those growth options.

For Rare, an international conservation nonprofit that set out to develop a funding model in 2010, the primary reason for creating a funding model was to fuel growth. The $12-million organization had developed an effective program model for operating social marketing campaigns to support conservation efforts, which it had tested with encouraging results in numerous countries. Rare's senior management team was ready to scale up the organization's efforts and expand to new countries. We will follow Rare's journey throughout this guide.

Organize your resources

Navigating the six steps will require a considerable investment of time and energy from individuals across your organization. To help coordinate this undertaking, we suggest developing a project workplan.

See **Appendix A** on page 47 for a sample workplan.

The team

Start by identifying a project lead (typically a senior staff member, such as the director of development), as you would with any major initiative. This individual will be accountable for managing the overall process. Your lead then should determine which person or team will tackle each of the six steps. Some steps, such as the analysis of your current approach to funding (Step 1), will require more senior contributors. Others, such as peer research (Step 2) may lend themselves to involving more junior members of the organization (or a summer MBA intern). Throughout the process, your organization's chief executive officer (CEO) or executive director (ED) will play a critical role in supporting the project lead's efforts.

The timeline

Once the roles are set, estimate how long each step will take and develop an overall project timeline. Consider using the aforementioned sample workplan as a starting point for your estimates. The entire process should require no more than four months of sustained effort. If it stretches out significantly longer, you're likely to lose momentum and have a harder time staying on track.

The steering committee

Most organizations also find it helpful to create a steering committee made up of senior staff from all parts of the organization and perhaps key board members. While some members may be more involved than others, this advisory group will review, provide feedback on, and approve the work done for each step in the process. Schedule periodic steering committee meetings (ideally one towards the end of each of the six steps) as soon as you establish your project timeline. Not only will doing so ensure that ample time is blocked off on members' calendars, but it will also serve to establish internal deadlines that will help keep the project on track.

In review: Key questions to consider when getting started

- Why are you interested in learning more about prospective funding models? What is your ultimate goal for this process?
- What are your organization's short-term and long-term goals? What revenue will you need to meet those goals?
- Where is there disagreement or lack of clarity in your organization around those goals? How might you address these issues before kicking off the funding models work?
- Are you clear on the roles and responsibilities your staff will play as you work to establish a funding model for your organization? Are these individuals able to commit the time and energy to complete the process within the desired time frame?

Step 1:
Analyze your current approach to funding

With funding models the way forward starts with a look back. This step may seem superfluous at first blush. After all, you already know a great deal about how your organization raises money. But stepping back and reflecting on the relative strengths and weaknesses of that approach is essential if you want to end up with a funding model that works for your organization.

Here's why: Adopting a new funding model will undoubtedly require new capabilities—in fundraising, performance measurement, reporting, and sometimes even program design and delivery. However, if these new capabilities are too far from your current ones, your odds of success may be lower. While external research can tell you which funding models are most promising in the abstract, only an in-depth understanding of your own organization can tell you which could work for you.

There's also the danger that some of what your organization believes about its current funding strategy is wrong. Consider the experience of Love Learning,[1] an education nonprofit that thought tours of its diagnostic learning clinics were key to getting individuals to fund the organization. The group was so convinced of the power of site visits that it spent a disproportionate amount of time arranging tours. And it planned to build more clinics, in part to enhance its ability to raise funds. However, when the group examined the share of total funding that came from donors who were motivated by clinic visits, it learned that it was a startlingly low percentage. With this knowledge, the group abandoned its plans to build more clinics and refocused its fund development efforts on the aspects of its work that truly were driving donors to give.

So use this opportunity to take a deliberate look at your organization's funding approach with a critical eye. By the end of this step in the process, you should be able to:

- Articulate which sources make up your revenue base, with an understanding of how reliable those sources are.

---

1 Organization's name has been disguised

- Understand who your key funding decision makers are and what motivates them.
- Summarize the strengths and weaknesses of your organization's fundraising capabilities.

You may find (as many nonprofits do) that your organization does not have a particularly strategic approach to funding. Perhaps you run after funding opportunities as they arise. Maybe your funding is idiosyncratic, varying considerably from year to year. These funding self-assessment results are fairly common and a fine place to start. Knowing where your current funding approach is vulnerable will help you to select a model that improves on those weaknesses. And being honest with yourself at this stage is critical to reaching a realistic solution later in the process.

Analyze historical financials

Gather your organization's historical funding data. Examining five years of data will allow you to identify trends in your organization's approach to funding. With this information documented, you will be able to articulate clearly—to your board, staff, and future funders—what your current revenue streams are. This knowledge will serve as a basis for describing how you may want those revenue streams to change in the future.

One good way to go about this is to develop an Excel spreadsheet as follows:
- Collect detailed funding data for the past five years, using one row of your spreadsheet for each grant, donation, or fee-for-service category.
- Categorize each line by type of funding (e.g., individual contributions, foundation grants, corporate donations, government funding, earned income). Try to refine your categories even more—for example, by separating individual contributions into small versus large donors, or by distinguishing between federal, state, and local government funding.
- Sort your list by type of funding. You'll then see all corporate donations together, then foundation grants, and so on.
- Using Excel's chart function, translate your analysis into a simple visual so you can more easily see trends.

See **Appendix B** on page 49 for examples of what this output could look like.

Consider the following questions, which will help clarify the reliability of your current funding approach and spark some ideas for how you might build on it in the future:

What percentage of your ongoing costs is covered by renewable funding sources?

In general, a renewable source is one you believe, with a high level of confidence, will continue for at least the next three to five years. This could be a government contract you've secured for multiple years, with no signs that the funding agency plans to change its decision-making criteria. Or perhaps it's an individual donor, with a deep personal commitment to your organization's work, who has been writing you $10,000 checks annually for the last seven years. In contrast, a foundation grant for a specific initiative that's slated to end in two years would land squarely outside of this category. Some sources likely will fall in more of a gray area, so you'll need to make some judgment calls. We generally consider an organization to be in a relatively strong position if at least 70 percent of its revenues are renewable.

Across how many funders are funding sources spread?

Identify your major funders—big individual donors, foundations, government agencies, and the like. How many do you have today? How many do you expect to have three to five years from now, assuming you maintain your current funding approach? Ideally, your organization garners revenue from three or more major funders, thereby giving it a good chance of weathering the loss of one.

The skinny on diversification

Conventional wisdom long held that diversifying an organization's funding mix by tapping several types of funding (e.g., government, corporate, etc.) was the best way to achieve financial sustainability. Our research has not found this to be the case. Instead, very large nonprofits raise most of their money from one type of funding. Fast-growing mid-sized nonprofits rely heavily on one type of funding and strategically tap one or sometimes two others.

What explains this departure from conventional wisdom? Natural matches between a nonprofit's work and funder interests are simply too hard to come by. It's very hard to imagine the same program appealing deeply to government funders AND corporations AND foundations AND small donors AND high-net-worth individuals, given the varied motivations behind their funding decisions. Pursuing a scattershot approach to try to cultivate all of these groups typically translates to under-investing in each one, making it incredibly difficult to discern which ones are most promising—never mind achieve their full potential.

The case for broad diversification within a single type of funding—say by accessing several different government funding streams, or tapping multiple segments of individual donors—is much more compelling. Doing so brings the desired risk management benefits while still allowing nonprofits to build and leverage expertise in raising a particular type of funding.

What percentage of funding is restricted to non-core operations and programs?

A good indicator of your organization's financial health is your historical success in securing funds that are not restricted to programs and operations tangential to your impact goals (i.e., non-core activities). As general rule of thumb, we define an organization as being in a relatively strong position if no more than 30 percent of funds are restricted to non-core activities.

When Rare undertook this historical funding analysis, it confirmed that funding was primarily driven by a few high-net-worth individuals who were either on the board or closely connected to board members. Securing or failing to secure a gift from any one of these people had the potential to swing Rare's financial picture quite a bit; in fact, the organization's revenues had been choppy for the past few years. Happily, these loyal funders had been consistent supporters for years and did not place significant restrictions on their donations. Most of Rare's other funding, including government and foundation, had grown in recent years, but remained at relatively modest levels.

Understand the motivation of current funders

Knowing which funders are likely to give in the future starts with understanding why your current funders give. Identify the characteristics of your organization that motivate your most loyal donors. Speaking directly with your funders is often helpful here. Does your proven track record drive them? The specific population with whom you're working? Create a list of key characteristics that seem to be driving significant, sustainable dollars to your organization.

Based on that list of donor motivations, articulate clearly what differentiates your organization in the eyes of these funders. By getting really specific here, you'll be better able to evaluate whether your current positioning will appeal to potential future donors or whether you'll need to alter that positioning to attract the level of funding you've targeted.

Consider, for example, the motivations behind the donors of Susan G. Komen for the Cure, a leader in the breast cancer movement. This organization identified early on that the bedrock of its funding is small individual donors who have been affected by breast cancer, either directly or through a loved one, and who want to help combat the disease. Knowing its donors' motivations, Susan G. Komen for the Cure organizes local cancer walks in myriad communities, thereby creating tangible, local opportunities to contribute.

In contrast, Rare's main source of funding was a small group of affluent environmentalists who were impressed by the organization's focus on community-level conservation and its track record of proven environmental outcomes. While Rare believed there was an opportunity to increase the number of individual donors in the coming years, the leadership team worried that the organization might hit a "funding ceiling" with this donor segment.

Understand your organization's current fundraising capabilities

There are undoubtedly certain fundraising activities that your organization is quite good at, and other areas where you've had less experience or even made some missteps. Maybe your appeals to wealthy individual donors often have borne fruit, but your efforts to win (never mind manage) government contracts have fallen flat. Crystallizing this knowledge will help you to be honest about what funding sources your organization can realistically hope to secure and what organizational investments are necessary in order to do so.

The following questions can help you evaluate your organization's fundraising capabilities:

Does a single individual (such as the CEO or ED, or a board member) generate most of your organization's revenue, or is fundraising more institutionalized?
Think about how fundraising responsibilities historically have been spread. An organization that has raised most of its funds through a charismatic leader may need to consider the broader set of staff capabilities needed to access new and larger pools of funding.

What is your development team's current capacity?
Getting a sense of your development team's skills will help you select funding models that build on its existing capabilities. Different funding sources may require different skill sets. Someone who is successful at cultivating major donors may not be well suited to write complicated government grant proposals.

Workload is another important consideration. If development staff are flat-out pursuing your organization's current approach to funding (as so often is the case), adopting a new funding model likely will require reallocating staff time or hiring additional staff.

This sort of reflection proved powerful to the Rare team. It recognized that President and CEO Brett Jenks was spending an increasing amount of his time cultivating and managing donor relationships as the number of key funders grew—an unsustainable trend. To support the organization's desired growth, the team knew that senior program leaders and the development team would need to assume greater fundraising responsibilities. Rare also observed that development staff were primarily set up to work with high-net-worth individuals and did not have deep expertise in raising other types of funds, such as government grants.

Share what you've learned with key internal stakeholders

Now that you've developed a clear picture of your organization's approach to funding, consider how widely it's understood throughout your organization. Can board members and staff accurately describe your approach? If not, take the time to familiarize them with what you have learned. To have productive conversations about the future and ultimately gain support for your future funding model, all parties need to know where you stand now.

Determine which funding sources are most attractive to explore further

Building on your clearer sense of your organization's current approach to funding, take some time to brainstorm which funding sources may be a good fit going forward. Be expansive in your thinking, as subsequent steps of this guide will provide ample opportunity to pressure test your ideas.

Rare's management team surfaced a number of ideas at this stage. Maybe Rare could grow by identifying several more large donors. Or by focusing on cities where it did not have a fundraising presence. Or by targeting a different profile of individual donor, such as those that make small gifts. All of these options made the brainstorming list. What about government funding? Rare had a small amount of it but the team knew that other organizations in its space were getting more. Though Rare did not have much experience landing and managing government contracts, this idea made the list. And given the team's past experience with foundation and corporate funding, it decided to keep these options on the table for now as well.

> ### In review: Key questions to consider when analyzing your current approach to funding
>
> - What are the biggest limitations of our current funding approach? Which of these are the highest priorities to address with our new funding model?
> - What inspires our most loyal funders to support us?
> - What are our organization's strengths and weaknesses when it comes to revenue generation? Which of these can we address easily (e.g., hiring one new development person if the team is stretched too thin)? Which are harder to change (e.g., building an entirely new skill set in development staff)?
> - Can key stakeholders—such as our board and senior management team—clearly articulate our funding approach? If not, what steps can we take to provide greater clarity before discussing future funding model options?
> - Which funding sources are we interested in researching further? Why do we think each source may be promising?

Step 2: Learn from the funding approaches of peer organizations

Now it's time to look at the funding approaches of peer organizations—ideally, peers that have been even more successful than you at securing funds. This research, combined with the ideas that grew out of your Step 1 diagnostic, ultimately will help you identify an initial set of funding models for consideration.

Some of you may be thinking, "My organization is unusual, maybe even unique. What if we require a unique funding model?" That reasoning is in fact why many nonprofit leaders balk at peer research. It's true that nothing exists before it has happened for the first time, but true first times don't happen nearly as often as we'd like. So while creating a never-seen-before funding model is sometimes possible, the truth is that doing so is generally far more difficult and less certain. It's hard to bet mission success on such things.

You also may ask yourself whether a peer's funding approach is worth emulating. Who's to say, after all, that it's any better than yours is? Selecting organizations that exhibit some signs of success, such as recent growth or endorsements from your contacts in the field, is definitely a good idea. Rest assured, however, that in Step 3 you'll be doing a good deal of pressure testing and homing in on only those that are sustainable and replicable.

By the end of this step, you should be able to:
- List specific organizations that may serve as potential funding strategy role models.
- Describe the essential characteristics of their approaches to funding.
- Understand how differences between these organizations and your own affect the relevance of their funding strategies.

Identify a small group of peer organizations

When you think about your organization's peer group, your mind probably first goes to organizations that are similar to your own in terms of *issue focus* (e.g., disease eradication, college access) and *size* (as measured by revenue). These aspects are in fact two of the most important to consider. Issue area is a primary determinant of the types of funders that will support a given organization.

Sources for researching peer organizations

When developing your list of peer organizations, start by mining your personal knowledge and brainstorming with your staff, board members, and funders. Then reach out to local experts, foundations, and associations that focus on your organization's issue area. A quick literature scan can also be productive and is often a good way to get beyond the usual suspects. Articles in broad-based publications like *The Chronicle of Philanthropy* or domain-specific ones such as *Youth Today* may point you to peers on the national scene. Searching Guidestar.org or CharityNavigator.org by field, budget size, and geography may also yield possibilities. Case studies on nonprofit organizations are another option, with sources including business school publications as well as our own website (www.bridgespan.org).

Once you've identified your peer group and you're ready to learn about its funding approaches, start by checking the organizations' websites and annual reports (if available). The odds are good that you'll find at least some basic financial information, and sometimes much more than that—such as press releases describing each major gift. The organizations' websites may also give you a sense for which donors they're targeting. For example, a peer that taps corporate funds may have corporate volunteer information on its website. One that relies on large individual donations may have guidance about charitable bequests. If you come up short with these sources, the organizations' 990 forms will provide funding information at a high level (i.e., public revenue, private contributions, and earned revenue). Foundationcenter.org and Guidestar.org both allow you to search for 990 forms free of charge.

After mining these public sources, you will likely want to speak with people at the peer organizations themselves. Having direct or indirect connections with these folks is ideal, but we've seen cold calls work as well—particularly when reaching out to nonprofits with which your organization would not compete directly for funds (for example, a nonprofit that provides a similar service but in a different geography, or one that taps similar types of funding but in pursuit of a different issue area). For some practical tips for conducting these conversations, see the sidebar, "Best practices for peer benchmarking interviews." on page 19.

Likewise, size matters—but that's not to say that you should only look to organizations that are roughly the same size as your own. If growth is a desired goal, the funding approaches used by organizations of your target size will likely be more informative. And regardless of your growth ambitions, choosing larger peers also tends to reveal more organizations that are more successful at fundraising than is yours.

Consider the experience of Rare. Because growth was the goal, Rare immediately started with the largest and best-known international conservation organizations, including The Nature Conservancy and Conservation International. Next, Rare added peer organizations that were comparable in size, such as the Rainforest Alliance and the African Wildlife Foundation. To round out this group, it included

What if your organization has few direct peers?

If your organization focuses on an uncommon program niche, you may have few (if any) natural peers—heightening the need to get creative in identifying nonprofits from which you can learn.

This was the case for HopeLab, which develops fun, effective technologies to drive positive health behavior in chronically-ill young people. An example is its Re-Mission video game, designed to give young cancer patients a sense of power and control over their disease by allowing them to "blast away" at cancer cells and scientifically proven to improve treatment adherence. HopeLab's leaders identified only one direct peer—Benetech, which incubates sustainable technology solutions for social needs and relies heavily on government support. They knew they'd need to look more broadly for inspiration.

HopeLab's leaders began their search by hypothesizing which types of funding could one day be at the heart of the organization's funding model. They then identified nonprofits known to specialize in cultivating those sources. For example, they researched KaBOOM! (which helps communities build playgrounds) for insight on raising corporate funds, Harvard EdLabs (which conducts education R&D focused on closing the achievement gap) for foundation support, and the Make-A-Wish Foundation (which grants wishes for children with life-threatening medical conditions) for individual donations.

After learning about the keys to these organizations' successful development efforts and comparing those factors to HopeLab's development capabilities and vision for impact, they found a closer fit with the approaches for raising government and foundation funds, and decided to research their applicability in more depth.

a few well-known environmental organizations that addressed issues beyond conservation, such as Natural Resources Defense Council (NRDC).

Your first pass at identifying a peer group will likely result in a list of organizations with which you are quite familiar. But looking beyond the usual suspects can often bring fresh ideas. Strive to include at least two or three organizations that you don't know well. These organizations are often ones with which you have some common bond, but also some significant differences. Perhaps you work on different issues but cultivate the same type of funding (e.g., high-net-worth individuals), or pursue a similar programmatic approach to achieving your mission (e.g., advocacy, direct service, lobbying), or focus on similar target beneficiaries for your services, or serve a similar geography (e.g., a specific city or state, a similarly sized city, a rural area). If your organization focuses on a unique program niche, you may have fewer "natural" peers to study. If that is the case, you may need to select more nontraditional peers.

For Rare, branching out meant focusing on organizations that excelled in raising funds from high-net-worth individuals. In addition to its environmental peers, Rare also included education nonprofit Teach For America and international-microfinance leader Opportunity International in its benchmark set. Both organizations were known to have developed exceptionally strong individual fundraising approaches.

Determine the essential characteristics of peer approaches to funding

For each peer, first identify the types of funding on which the organization relies. Then, for its top one or two types of funding, probe deeper to learn more about specific funding sources and tactics. Focusing on the leading sources is often a productive way to guide your work, given that most funding models hinge on a single type of funding.

Understanding peers' overall funding mix

Aim to find the last five years of total revenue, broken down by each type of funding (i.e., government, foundation, individual, corporate, and earned revenue). Keep in mind, however, that historical revenues may be difficult to find, and data may come in less detail than you'd ideally like. (See the sidebar, on page 20, "The art and science of benchmarking.") Be sure to understand what the organization's top one or two types of funding are. Even if you are unable to build a detailed break-out of all the organization's funding, try to develop at least a directional sense (e.g., 70 to 80 percent of funds come from government sources, with the rest mainly from individuals and foundations). And if you end up relying heavily on estimates, aim to consult more than one source and cross-check what you learn from each one.

Probing deeper on the leading types of funding

Now it's time to really understand those top types of funding. Your goal here is to develop a sense of the individual streams of funding involved—specifically how many discrete sources the peer organization taps, what those sources are, and what tactics it uses to cultivate them. This knowledge will give you insight into key characteristics of the organization's funding approach—namely who its main funding decision makers are and (given that, generally speaking, more sources translate to greater reliability) how reliable its funding base is.

Consider the following probing questions for the peer organization, depending on which type of funding you're investigating:

- *Government:* What is the organization's mix of federal, state, and local funding? Which grants, contracts, earmarks, and/or government agencies does it tap?

Best practices for peer benchmarking interviews

- **Identify the right contact point:** Keep in mind that the most senior person isn't necessarily the most knowledgeable. Often a member of the development team is a good bet.
- **Be upfront:** Never misrepresent yourself or the reason for your call. Introduce yourself and your organization, and tell your contacts why you need their help for an important project.
- **Make connections:** If you've never worked together before, mention how you found them. Whether you were connected through a mutual friend, or you admire a recently launched program, letting them know will help put you both at ease.
- **Make it a two-way street:** If you're ready and willing to share information about your organization's own development efforts and to discuss common challenges, chances are peers will be more open.
- **Share results:** Contacts may appreciate hearing the results of your broader benchmarking analysis when it is complete. Just be sure to clarify upfront with everyone you interview what degree of confidentiality they expect.
- **Respect their time:** Before you call, make sure the information you are asking for isn't displayed on the front page of their website or readily available through other public sources. And make sure you know exactly what you'd like to get out the call, so you can avoid having to go back to them for more information.

- *Individual:* Do the organization's funds come largely from a handful of wealthy philanthropists, or do they consist of many small donations from the general public? (One quick way to figure out this detail is to determine what percentage of the funds comes from the top five donors.) If small donations are key, are they mainly coming from direct mail, special events, online giving, or some combination of these?

- *Foundation*: Does the organization rely on one or two foundations for the majority of its revenue, or does it draw revenue more evenly from a larger set of foundations? Do these funds come largely from standard grants or from growth capital grants?
- *Corporate*: Do the majority of the organization's corporate funds originate from one or two companies, or does it tap a broad set of businesses? Are the funds in the form of in-kind giving, employee matching programs, or sponsorship and co-branding initiatives? Is philanthropy or corporate goals the primary motivation behind the funds?
- *Earned revenue*: Do these revenues take the form of fees for service or membership fees? If fees for service, does the organization rely on a few key contracts or a broader base? If membership fees, what is its membership base?

Don't worry if you can't find detailed data to inform these questions. Often developing just a general sense for the answers is enough to get a good handle on the peer organization's approach to funding.

Soon after starting the peer research process, Rare confirmed what it had known anecdotally—that many international conservation organizations relied on both individual and government funding. Upon reviewing the African Wildlife Foundation's historical financials, for example, Rare noticed that the organization had both a consistent individual funding base with a number of large individual donors and steadily growing government funding streams from a variety of sources, including the United States Agency for International Development (USAID) and European governments.

The art and science of benchmarking

In an ideal world, you would be able to follow the directions in this section step by step, gathering precise and detailed information from your peer organizations. In reality, though, much of this information can be relatively hard to come by. (Believe us—we've learned this lesson first hand!) Don't feel discouraged if you're not able to get all the pieces of information in as much detail as suggested in this guide. And when quantitative data is not available, consider using qualitative information to form estimates. Focus on understanding the underlying themes and information, and be flexible in considering alternative outputs to those we've offered as samples here.

Identify key programmatic, financial, and governance differences

By now you should have a fairly good understanding of each peer organization's funding approach. Next comes figuring out how applicable those approaches are to your organization. Identify any key differences between these peer organizations and your own that may limit your ability to follow in their footsteps. What you're after are points of difference that contribute to their funding success.

The attributes you used during your scan for peer organizations—such as issue focus, programmatic approach, target beneficiaries, and geography—are relevant here, given that they're all things that could factor into why a given funder would support one of your peer organizations but not your own. For example, Rare recognized that funders that were likely to support international conservation were different from funders that supported Opportunity International, which focuses on poverty alleviation. Nevertheless, Rare was able to glean some important lessons about how Opportunity International helped its US-based funders develop a strong sense of affiliation with communities that were thousands of miles away.

Delving deeper, here are a few additional areas on which to probe peers for differences:

- *Organizational structure*: Is the organization configured as a stand-alone entity, as a network itself, or as part of a broader network? Within networks, how independently run is each location? A national network may be in strong position to tap both national and local funding with combined fundraising efforts of the national office and its affiliates. And an organization that's part of a larger network may have fundraising support from the central office.
- *Age and/or brand recognition*: When was the organization established? How well-known is its brand? A more established and better-known organization may have an easier time attracting some types of donors, particularly individuals and corporations. Government funders also tend to favor the relative safety of established organizations when awarding grants and contracts.
- *Magnitude of development resources*: What is the organization's budget for development? How many employees and volunteers does it engage in fundraising activities? This information will give you a sense of the resources needed to implement the peer's funding approach at a similar scale. Some funding approaches may require more investment than you're willing to make.
- *Results*: Does the organization share its outcome data? Has it tested its results through formal trials by an evaluation expert? Are any of its current funders known for setting a high bar for results? Greater rigor in outcome data can help differentiate an organization from others, giving it an advantage in fundraising. Here we're talking about going beyond measuring outputs (e.g., number of kids served) to documenting results (e.g., number of kids who graduate from high school). Some funders, including many foundations and government agencies, strongly favor organizations with sophisticated systems for tracking results.

- *Size and prominence of board*: How many members make up the organization's board? How prominent are they? Does a separate advisory board provide additional support? How much are board members expected to contribute and/or raise annually? Board members account for a large percentage of overall revenue at some organizations. Without a complete overhaul of your own board, it may be hard to replicate the peer's approach.

As you collect this information, start forming your hypotheses on the extent to which the differences you uncover represent either a fundraising advantage or disadvantage relative to your own organization, like Rare did when considering the applicability of Opportunity International's approach. Note that coming up with this information may very well be a challenge, especially if you're limited to secondary sources. You likely will need to be flexible and a bit creative in creating a profile for each organization.

In review: Key questions to consider when learning from the approaches of peer organizations

- What are the main types of funding upon which peer organizations rely?
- Who are the main entities these organizations need to convince to support their work? And what appears to motivate those donors to give?
- What differences between our organization and peers may limit our ability to pursue their funding approaches?

Step 3:
Identify and narrow your
range of funding model options

By now you've likely learned a great deal about how peer organizations get their money. "But which among all these possibilities," you may be asking yourself, "are funding models?" Exactly the question! Your next step is to see if you can identify any funding models your organization might want to replicate. As you recall, we define a funding model as a *methodical and institutionalized approach to building a reliable revenue base.*

Chances are that some of the organizations in your peer group will have clear funding models. Some will be more idiosyncratic in their funding approaches. The ones with funding models are the gems here, as their funding approaches, by definition, are sustainable and replicable—just what you're after.

By the end of this step, you should be able to:
- List the funding models used by peer organizations.
- Decide which of those models are most applicable to your organization.

Identify the funding models
in use within your peer group

So how can you tell which peers have funding models and which ones don't? Consider the three defining characteristics of a funding model that we noted earlier—type of funding, funding decision makers, and funder motivation. Answer the following questions for each peer you researched:
- *Type of funding*: What are the organization's major types of funding?
- *Funding decision makers*: For each major type of funding, who determines how much funding is allocated to the organization?
- *Funder motivation*: Why do those decision makers choose to allocate funding to the organization?

If your answers to these questions are fuzzy, it's very likely that the peer does not in fact have a funding model. But if they're sharp and clear, the chances are good that it does—in which case you'll want to figure out which funding model it is. See if the three attributes match any documented nonprofit funding models, or if they constitute a new one.

By "documented" we're referring to 10 nonprofit models we identified in our past research of very large organizations. [2] These 10 certainly are not the only funding models in existence, but they're a good place to start. Descriptions of these models, complete with their funding type, decision makers, and motivation, are included in Figure 2.

Figure 2

Funding model	Description	Categorization	Tactical tools	Example organizations
Heartfelt Connector	• Mission has broad appeal • Benefits often touch the lives of the funder's family and friends	• Type: Individuals • Decision maker: Many individuals • Motivation: Altruism	• Special events • Direct mail • Corporate sponsorship	• Medical research (Susan G. Komen Foundation) • Environment (NRDC)
Beneficiary Builder	• Mission initially attracts individuals pursuing, and paying for, specific individual benefits • Mission creates a strong individual connection through the delivery of the benefit	• Type: Individuals • Decision maker: Many individuals • Motivation: Self-interest followed by altruism	• Earned income/fees • Major gifts	• Universities (Princeton University) • Hospitals (Cleveland Clinic)
Member Motivator	• Most benefits have a group orientation, creating an inherent community for fund-raising	• Type: Individuals • Decision maker: Many individuals • Motivation: Collective interest	• Membership • Fees • Special events • Major gifts • Direct mail	• Religious congregations (Saddleback Church) • Environment and conservation (National Wild Turkey Federation)
Big Bettor	• Majority of support comes from a few individuals or family foundations • Mission may be fulfilled within limited number of decades	• Type: Individuals/foundations • Decision maker: Few individuals • Motivation: Altruism	• Major gifts	• Medical research (The Stanley Medical Research Institute) • Environment (Conservation International)
Beneficiary Broker	• Individual beneficiaries decide how to spend the government benefit (i.e., charter school vouchers)	• Type: Government • Decision maker: Many individuals • Motivation: Self-interest	• Government reimbursement	• Health (E. Boston Neighborhood Health Center) • Housing (Metro. Boston Housing Partnership) • Employment (Peckham Vocational Industries)
Public Provider	• Services that are perceived as a core government responsibility are provided	• Type: Government • Decision maker: Administrators • Motivation: Collective interest	• Government contracts	• Human services (TMC) • International (Family Health International)
Policy Innovator	• Government funds are secured for a significant new approach to address a problem not currently viewed as a core government responsibility	• Type: Government • Decision maker: Policymakers • Motivation: Collective interest	• Legislative appropriation or earmark • Executive earmark • Government pilot program	• Human Services (Youth Villages) • Education (Communities in Schools)

2 To learn more about our research and the funding models we identified, see "Ten Nonprofit Funding Models," (*Stanford Social Innovation Review*, Spring 2009) on page 59.

Funding model	Description	Categorization	Tactical tools	Example organizations
Resource Recycler	• The nonprofit uses goods created in the market economy where there are surpluses (e.g., food) or where marginal costs to produce a product are low (e.g., pharmaceuticals)	• Type: Corporations • Decision maker: Few individuals • Motivation: Self-interest	• In-kind giving	• Food (Oregon Food Bank) • International (Ameri-Cares Foundation)
Market Maker	• A funder with some degree of self-interest and the ability to pay exists (for example, a health system buying blood)	• Type: Mixed • Decision maker: Many individuals (one side), few individuals (other side) • Motivation: Altruism (one side), self-interest (other side)	• Earned income/fees • Major gifts (corporate or individual)	• Health (American Kidney Fund) • Environment or conservation (The Trust for Public Land)
Local Nationalizer	• An issue that is a top local priority is addressed • That issue is common enough to exist in many localities nationwide	• Type: Mixed • Decision maker: Few individuals • Motivation: Altruism	• Major gifts • Special events	• Youth development (Big Brothers Big Sisters of America) • Education (Teach For America)

After studying its peers, Rare recognized that some did have clear funding models. For example, Conservation International's funding approach corresponded to the Big Bettor funding model. The organization's ability to identify locations around the world where protecting an area of land can have a significant effect on preserving global biodiversity helps it attract a small number of donors who are willing to contribute large amounts of money so they can have an important and lasting impact on protecting the Earth. And the African Wildlife Foundation, which manages extensive USAID contracts, matched the description of the Public Provider funding model. NRDC, with its sophisticated small gifts marketing program, fit the Heartfelt Connector mold.

You may find yourself thinking that some of your peer organizations embody more than one or two of these models. In fact, we frequently hear nonprofit leaders describe efforts to pursue three, four, or even more models. While not impossible theoretically, the odds of pulling off such a scattershot approach (i.e., making that many successful matches with donor motivations, developing the necessary capabilities to cultivate that many different types of funding well) are incredibly low. In our prior research on large organizations, the vast majority had one dominant funding model, a few had two, and none had three or more. Accordingly, it's far more likely that what you're observing is an idiosyncratic grab bag of funding approaches, rather than a collection of viable funding models. Tip-offs here include volatility in the organization's revenue mix or total amount of revenue over the five-year period you studied in Step 2.

Bear in mind that our list of 10 funding models is not comprehensive given that it's derived from studying organizations that have reached $50 million in annual revenues. A wider array of funding models applies for smaller nonprofits. So even though you don't yet have a match, you may still be dealing with a viable funding model.

For example, Rare observed that some peer organizations seemed to depend on support from a *network* of high-net-worth individuals. This approach did not meet the criteria of the Big Bettor model, with its traditional reliance on a *small number* of ultra high-net-worth individuals. And while it matched the Local Nationalizer model on the network dimension, a key point of departure existed: while the peers' funders supported overseas issues, Local Nationalizer funders focused on issues in their own communities. Nevertheless, from Rare's research and internal knowledge emerged a clear donor profile for individuals who funded international conservation efforts. So Rare kept this approach on the list, even though it was not one of the 10 established funding models.

More generally, you need to determine if the peer's funding approach is sustainable and replicable—the hallmarks of a funding model. (See Figure 3, "The funding model test.") Start by assessing its sustainability. How long has the organization been following the funding approach in question? If it's two years or less, its approach could very well be short term or opportunistic.

Figure 3

The funding model test

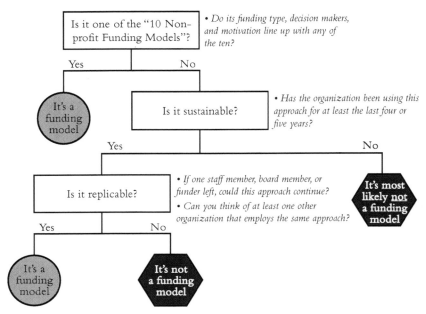

As for replicability, make sure that the organization's funding success isn't inextricably tied to a unique asset—such as a specific leader or board member, or an unmatched set of resources or capabilities. Additionally, take some time to see if you can think of any other organizations that use this model; if you can't, there is likely a reason.

Consider, for example, the Council of Chief State School Officers (CCSSO), a national membership organization of public officials that head departments of elementary and secondary education. CCSSO provides leadership, advocacy, and technical assistance on major educational issues. Most of its revenues come from foundations, but it doesn't fit the mold of the aforementioned foundation-driven (or wealthy individual-driven) Big Bettor model. CCSSO's decision makers include many foundation program officers who contract with CCSSO for specific projects, compared to the Big Bettor model, in which a small number of individuals provide grants altruistically to help the organization wipe out a societal problem within a foreseeable time frame.

Does CCSSO's approach constitute a funding model? The organization's revenues and revenue mix have been relatively stable at just under $25 million per year with consistent sources, making for a "yes" on sustainability. And since the foundations that contract with CCSSO do so primarily on the basis of the organization's expertise (rather than personal relationships, or some other hard-to-match attribute), it's reasonable to assume that a similarly-skilled organization could replicate its approach. In fact, nonprofit consulting organizations, such as The Bridgespan Group, and advocacy organizations such as the Center for Law and Social Policy, also use this funding model, which is akin to a business-to-business model.

Determine which peer funding models may be feasible for your organization

Now it's time to do an initial assessment to narrow down the list of peer funding models to those that seem like they could apply to your organization—ideally just two to four models. Doing so will allow you to focus on in-depth assessments of their pluses and minuses.

For each funding model on your short list, consider your organization's fit along the following dimensions:

- *The three defining characteristics of the model—type of funding, funder decision makers, funder motivations:* For the model's primary type(s) of funding, would your program model allow you to appeal successfully to the relevant decision makers, tapping into the same motivations that lay behind their funding of peer organizations? In order to do so, would you need to make any changes to your program model, such as adjusting existing programs, adding new ones, serving different beneficiaries, or expanding to new geographies? Would you be willing to make those changes?

- *Fund development capabilities:* Does your organization have the capabilities required to access the relevant sources of funds? For example, could you cultivate wealthy individual donors or manage the complexities of government contracting? If not, could you realistically develop those capabilities? Do you have the appetite for doing so?
- *Your funding model goals:* Will the funding model support the goals you laid out while working on the "getting ready" section of this guide? For example, can it get your organization to the size you aspire to achieve? (If the peers that use it are smaller than your target, it's quite possible that the funding model wouldn't get you to your desired size.)

See Figure 4 on page 29 for some more detailed questions tailored to the 10 funding models that are common in large organizations.

Two funding models were particularly prevalent in Rare's peer group: the Public Provider funding model and the aforementioned model that revolved around networks of high-net-worth individuals. Both clearly warranted further investigation.

Two other funding models—Big Bettor and Heartfelt Connector—were also represented in Rare's peer group, but with less frequency. Given that difference, Rare looked at them with an even more critical eye. Rare's social marketing wasn't the sort of approach that could eradicate a given environmental conservation issue in a relatively small number of years—the time frame and results Big Bettor donors look for—but rather was geared towards making continual progress over several years. Similarly, its science-based marketing efforts did not tend to evoke the emotional response in small individual donors that's characteristic of the Heartfelt Connector model. Rare decided to cross both of these models off its list. Rare's Senior Vice President of Strategy and Growth Martha Piper saw great value in this step, noting that, "One of the most helpful exercises was eliminating models we didn't want to pursue. We no longer needed to talk about mass mailings or other similar marketing tactics."

In review: Key questions to consider when identifying and narrowing your range of funding model options

- What is the range of funding models among our peer group?
- What is our organization's appetite for change from how things are done today?
- What are the main benefits of moving to the funding model in consideration? What might we lose?

Figure 4

Funding model	Key questions to assess the feasibility of a funding model
Heartfelt Connector	• Has a large cross section of people already shown that they will fund causes in this domain? • Can we communicate what is compelling about our nonprofit in a simple and concise way? • Does a natural avenue exist to attract and involve large numbers of volunteers? • Do we have, or can we develop, the capabilities to attempt broad outreach in even one geographic area?
Beneficiary Builder	• Does our mission create an individual benefit that is also perceived as an important social good? • Do individuals develop a deep loyalty to the organization in the course of receiving their individual benefit? • Do we have the infrastructure to reach out to beneficiaries in a scalable fashion?
Member Motivator	• Will our members feel that the actions of the organization are directly benefiting them, even if the benefit is shared collectively? • Do we have the ability to involve and manage our members in fundraising activities? • Can we commit to staying in tune with, and faithful to, our core membership, even if it means turning down funding opportunities and not pursuing activities that fail to resonate with our members?
Big Bettor	• Can we create a tangible and lasting solution to a major problem in a foreseeable time frame? • Can we clearly articulate how we will use large-scale funding to achieve our goals? • Are any of the wealthiest individuals or foundations interested in our issue and approach?
Beneficiary Broker	• Can we demonstrate to the government our superior ability to connect benefit or voucher holders with benefits, such as successful placement rates and customer satisfaction feedback? • Can we develop supplemental services that maximize the value of the benefit? • Can we attract enough clients/customers? • Can we master the government regulations and requirements needed to provide these benefits? • Can we find ways to raise money to supplement the fees we receive from the benefits program?
Public Provider	• Is our organization a natural match with one or more large, preexisting government programs? • Can we demonstrate that our organization will do a better job than our competitors? • Are we willing to take the time to secure contract renewals on a regular basis?
Policy Innovator	• Do we provide an innovative approach that surpasses the status quo (in impact and cost) and is compelling enough to attract government funders, which tend to gravitate toward traditional solutions? • Can we provide government funders with evidence that our program works? • Are we willing and able to cultivate strong relationships with government decision makers who will advocate change? • At this time, are there sufficient pressures on government to overturn the status quo?
Resource Recycler	• Are the products that we distribute likely to be donated on an ongoing basis? • Can we develop the expertise to stay abreast of trends in the industries that donate products to us, so we can prepare for fluctuations in donations? • Do we have a strategy for attracting the cash we'll need to fund operations and overhead?
Market Maker	• Is there a group of funders with a financial interest in supporting our work? • Are there legal or ethical reasons why having a nonprofit deliver the services would be more appropriate? • Do we already have a trusted program and brand name?
Local Nationalizer	• Does our cause address an issue that local leaders consider a high priority, and is this issue compelling in communities across the country? • Does expanding our organization into other communities fulfill our mission? • Can we replicate our model in other communities? • Are we committed to identifying and empowering high-performing leaders to run local branches of our organization in other communities?

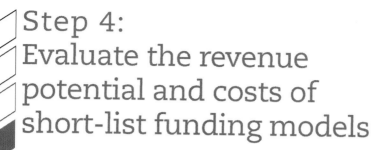

Step 4: Evaluate the revenue potential and costs of short-list funding models

Now that you have developed a short list of potential funding models, you'll need to take an in-depth look at how realistic those options are for your organization from a cost/benefit perspective, building on your initial assessment in Step 3. Here, you'll get a directional sense for both how much revenue you reasonably could expect to access through each model and what investments in your organization's programs, staff, and systems would be required. This knowledge will put you in a good position to make an informed decision about which funding model(s) to pursue.

By the end of this step, you should be able to:
- Understand the funding available for each funding model on your short list, as well as the competitive environment for that money.
- Describe how likely your organization is to secure significant dollars through each model.
- Estimate the investments your organization would need to make to pursue each model.

Understand the funding available

There's a wealth of readily-available information that can help you understand the revenue potential of a given funding model. And with your options now down to just a few models, you can conduct your research in a targeted way. For each of the funding models on your short list, focus on the leading type(s) of funding on which the funding model is built, using the following questions to guide your efforts:
- *Which funding sources should your organization prioritize?* Here you'll want to get specific. Perhaps the priority is the few dozen high-net-worth donors with an affinity for your issue area, or a particular federal funding stream that aligns well with your services and target beneficiaries. If peers have been particularly successful with a source, chances are you'll want to pay close attention to it, too.

- *How many total dollars are awarded annually through each of your prioritized funding sources?* This information will allow you to see if the dollars associated with the funding model match the scale of your organization's size aspirations. If, for example, you hope to secure $10 million annually from foundations, but total foundation giving to your issue area only averages $20 million each year, chances are you'll be hard pressed to hit your fundraising target.

- *How competitive is the environment for these funding sources?* Understand which other organizations are going after the same funding sources. This will help you to gauge how difficult securing it would be—and thus how much of the funding your organization could reasonably expect to access. Would you be one of the first organizations to access a source of funding? Are you competing with many similar nonprofits? Another important indicator is the average grant or contribution size relative to the total dollars awarded; the more concentrated the opportunities, the more pressure on your organization to stack up favorably against competing organizations.

Beyond mining your previous peer benchmarking work, website research and expert interviews can both be effective approaches here. With government funding, for example, you may want to start by canvassing websites such as Grants.gov and those of relevant state government departments, and then filling in any important knowledge gaps by interviewing the relevant public officials. For foundation funding, you'll likely want to spend some time on the Foundation Center's online database, which will allow you to determine the total foundation giving to your issue area and to pinpoint foundations that seem to be a good fit based on their giving history. (For more detail on how to research the funding available for various funding models, please see **Appendix C** on page 53.)

> ## "False positives" on government funding websites
> Early scans of government websites often turn up long lists of potentially promising grants and contracts. The reality is that closer examination undoubtedly will reveal that the majority are not in fact relevant. Digging into their requirements is essential to getting a true read on your prospects for government funding.

By way of example, consider Rare's experience exploring the potential of the "Public Provider" funding model. One of the public funding sources Rare's management team researched was USAID, having noted that several peer organizations received USAID contract funding. Canvassing USAID.gov gave them a detailed understanding of how much USAID funding had gone to international conservation over the past several years in the countries where Rare had (or was planning to establish) programs. The team then interviewed contacts at peer organizations and USAID to gauge how much funding an organization like Rare could reasonably expect to access. USAID emerged as a promising funding source that could help Rare achieve its growth goals.

Rare also sought to understand the market for high-net-worth individuals who give to environmental issues. The management team referenced the Center on Philanthropy's "Million Dollar List," a list of individuals who have made gifts of more than $1 million, segmented by issue area. It complemented that data by interviewing contacts at a number of peer organizations. Through this research, Rare identified promising pockets of high-net-worth individuals living in a handful of urban areas beyond the small geographic area where Rare's current donors clustered.

Determine the strength of your organization's fit

Beyond the competitive environment for funds, another big variable is how well your organization fits with that funding model. Chances are the fit is at least pretty good, given that the model has made your short list. But the better the fit, the further you're likely to get. Consider three factors:

- *Funding motivation*: How well does your organization's work align with the motivations behind the key funding decision makers associated with the funding model?
- *Requirements to access funding*: Could your organization realistically satisfy the eligibility rules, programmatic requirements, and necessary processes to qualify for this funding source?
- *Peer funding recipients*: How is your organization similar (or dissimilar) to other nonprofits that have been particularly successful in securing this funding source in the past? (Your peer research from Step 2 will be helpful here.)

When Rare's management team evaluated the organization's fit with USAID funding, for example, it reasoned that Rare possessed the same qualifications that made its peer organizations successful at accessing the funding—conservation programs with proven results in countries where USAID invested in biodiversity. The team confirmed that Rare would be a viable candidate by interviewing peers and researching the qualification criteria for USAID funding outlined on USAID's website.

Estimate the required investments

You now have a good handle on the upside associated with the funding models on your short list. But as the old adage goes "nothing in life is free." Adopting a new funding model often requires investments in programs, staff, IT systems, and communication materials, with some funding models requiring higher levels of investment than others. That level of investment is an important consideration when deciding which model to pick, not the least because things that are harder to do often bring a higher risk of failure.

Programs

Program investments may be a must for some funding sources, particularly in the government realm. Sometimes these changes take the form of adapting your existing programs to meet the funding source's standards (say by extending the length of time you work with a given program recipient). Or you may even need to introduce an entirely new program, or serve a different group of beneficiaries.

Tread carefully when exploring program investments, though. The strongest organizations tend to be the ones that remain focused on what they do best. Any changes you decide to make to your program offering should improve both your likelihood of securing funding and, more importantly, your ability to make progress on the issue you care about. BELL, the after-school and summer-learning organization we discussed in the introduction, had to make several hard decisions involving program investments. Accessing Title I SES funding would require it to make only modest changes to its programming. In contrast, several other funding streams that targeted related but different program outcomes, such as early child advocacy, would have required much more substantive changes—changes BELL elected not to pursue for fear doing so would compromise the organization's mission.

In the case of Rare, research of USAID and other public funding opportunities revealed a sufficient number of contracts that aligned with Rare's existing approach, so it did not have to pursue program modifications. It would forgo the opportunities that were beyond the organization's current program focus and target countries.

Personnel

New capabilities and more staff time are often required to source and manage the funds associated with a new model. You may find that you need to create and fill new roles, evolve the CEO's role in development, replace existing staff who lack the skills the new funding model demands, add more staff in areas where you're capacity-constrained, and/or provide additional training. These personnel investments may not all fall directly into the development arm of your organization. For example, you may need to:

- Add marketing staff if you plan to pursue an individual funding strategy;
- Enhance your organization's performance measurement capabilities if new funders require increased reporting;
- Develop new skills among your program staff if you're planning to make significant programmatic changes; and/or
- Allocate significant executive director time if you intend to cultivate relationships with new foundations.

Rare spent a fair bit of time figuring out the personnel implications of pursuing public funding, given that its development team was built around individual fundraising. Through interviews with peers and public funding contacts, Rare learned that organizations that successfully accessed key sources of public funding had a number of key development staff who specialized in cultivating those sources. While Rare had some government funding, it realized from its work in Step 1 that the team was not well equipped to deal with public funding contracts at any meaningful level of scale. Rare recognized that hiring development staff with these skills would be a necessary investment, but decided that the potential funding available outweighed the cost of bringing on new staff.

IT systems

New funding models often place greater demands on IT systems, particularly related to performance measurement. Your existing data management systems may not be sufficient to support the reporting requirements of new funders and/or to provide you with the information you need to manage your growing organization effectively. Additionally, stepped-up efforts to cultivate individual donors may require an enhanced online donor management system.

Rare had learned from its public funding research that organizations with demonstrable results had the advantage. Fortunately Rare had already invested in a performance monitoring system that would support the associated reporting requirements.

Communication materials

New funding models may make it more important to have top-notch communication materials to support external relations and marketing. Perhaps a more compelling annual report will be important in cultivating individual donors. Or maybe your grant applications need more depth if you're to win new government contracts or foundation grants.

Rare learned that the Natural Resources Defense Council's (NRDC's) small-gifts marketing campaigns were more successful when its mailings included clear visuals of "charismatic" animals like polar bears and details of how contributions would support efforts to protect them. While Rare did not believe that it should go after the same type of donors that NRDC generally sought, learning about NRDC's communications strategy led Rare to consider how it might need to invest in this area.

For more information on understanding the required investment, please see the sidebar on page 36, "Questions to gauge the required investment."

Questions to gauge the required investment

The following questions can help you get your arms around the investments required to adopt a given funding model. Your peer research can come in handy again here, illuminating some of the likely areas of investment.

Programs

- Would we need to adapt our current programs in a major way (e.g., offer additional services, modify existing services)?
- Would we need to introduce new programs?
- Would we need to target different beneficiaries?

Personnel

- Would we need to create and fill new roles (e.g., hiring a government relations expert for the first time)?
- Would the CEO's role need to evolve? How would we need to support that evolution (e.g., bringing in a COO to free up CEO time to lead priority development efforts)?
- Would we need to rehire for existing roles (e.g., if a current program director lacks the skills to adapt to the new funding strategy)?
- Would we need to hire more staff to give us sufficient resources to pursue additional funding?
- Would we need to provide staff with additional training?

IT systems

- Would we need to enhance our data management systems to support our performance management and reporting efforts?
- Would we need to improve our donor management system?

Communication materials

- Would we need to develop new marketing materials?
- Would we need to engage outside specialists to improve our grant applications?

In review: Key questions to consider when evaluating the revenue potential and costs of short-list funding models

- How many dollars can our organization realistically capture, given how many others provide services similar to ours and our ability to differentiate?
- How might we need to adapt our programs, staff, IT systems, and communications to meet the requirements of a particular funding model? What are we *not* willing to change?

Step 5: Select funding models to implement

Now it's time to select one or two funding models to implement. There's no math formula or complex decision rule to dictate your answer here. You just have to draw upon all your hard work from Steps 1 through 4, use your best judgment, and make the call.

You may be wondering why only one or two. Why not pursue all options that seem promising? In short, implementing more than two carries a high risk of over-taxing your management and development staff. Succeeding with a funding

Don't throw the baby out with the bath water

Developing a funding model does *not* mean that your organization should relinquish existing funding sources that don't fit with the new model. In fact, those sources often play complementary roles on a sustained basis by, for example, advancing a particular program or organizational objective for which the new model is not well suited or by providing a buffer against funding volatility.

For example, while Susan G. Komen for the Cure derives the bulk of its revenue from small, individual donations, corporate sponsorships for its breast cancer walks constitute a healthy secondary source. And one of Rare's important secondary sources is foundation support: Beyond financial contributions, foundations provide the organization with highly valuable thought partnership on programs and also play a critical role in validating Rare's program for other donors.

Rather than abandoning efforts to cultivate existing sources, pursuing a funding model involves focusing your next set of investments of time and staff on funding sources that are highly aligned with the model. The new sources will become the growth engines for the future, while revenues from current sources may remain roughly steady and thus represent a declining share of your organization's growing funding base.

model hinges on getting really good at cultivating its characteristic funding sources, so splitting staff in too many directions is bound to undermine your efforts. And when none of the models shows the hoped-for results (as will likely be the case), you'll be hard pressed to discern which failed due to poor fit versus underinvestment.

On the flip side, you may be wondering why you should consider implementing two instead of just one. After all, our research has shown that large nonprofits tend to have only one funding model. The issue here is uncertainty. Despite all your research, at this stage it may still be difficult for you to really know which model will work best for your organization. If so, before you fully commit to one, consider trying out the two most promising options to see which has the most promise.

Have one or two strong front-runners already emerged as you've navigated Steps 1 through 4? If so, reach out to key stakeholders on your board and staff to make sure they'd support the decision to pursue and invest in building them.

Do three or more funding models still seem appealing? Well, then it's time to make some tough choices to further narrow down your list. Compare each model that remains on your list across the dimensions you investigated in Step 4—the magnitude of the funding available, your organization's ability to access that funding, and the investments required to do so. You may want to go so far as to develop a simple scorecard whereby your steering committee could rate each funding model option on these three dimensions.

When Rare decided to pick a funding model or two to implement, its management team remained confident that a funding strategy anchored around public funders had high potential. The team also recognized that the organization was not yet positioned to maximize those funding streams because it did not have the right development staff in place. Accordingly, Rare's leadership team and board decided that over the next three years the organization would strengthen its long-time individual giving strategy while also pursuing the Public Provider funding model. By investing in both its current capabilities and its long-term funding aspirations, Rare's leadership had a plan to strengthen the organization's short-term and long-term outlook. There was a great deal of energy and enthusiasm behind these decisions, with Senior Vice President of Strategy and Growth Martha Piper noting that, "Doing the analysis and using the data enabled us to make choices with confidence."

In review: Key questions to consider when selecting models to implement

- What funding model options are most likely to help us achieve the goals that we set for ourselves at the onset of the process?
- Would our board and other stakeholders support the investments required to develop this funding model over time?

Step 6: Develop an implementation plan

Congratulations—you've made it to the sixth and final step! Your goal now is to make your funding model plans actionable by developing an implementation plan.

As we mentioned at the outset of this guide, creating your funding model will not happen overnight—or even in six months, for that matter. Building the right capabilities, finding the right people, and forging the right relationships take time. Funding models typically require two to three years to take hold. A good implementation plan is an invaluable resource as your organization navigates that journey.

Your implementation plan will give your staff and board a shared vision of where your organization is heading. It will spell out the intermediate steps required to get you from your current funding approach to your desired funding model(s), thereby helping to coordinate staff efforts and increasing the odds that your efforts are successful. It will also establish clear milestones and a learning agenda, making it easier to track progress and make course corrections.

By the end of this step you should be able to:
- Describe in detail the investments your organization will need to make.
- Create a step-by-step plan for making those investments and implementing your funding model.
- Understand the communication and monitoring commitments required to keep your implementation efforts on track.

Crystallize priority investments

In Step 4 you identified the key program, personnel, IT system, and communications investments required to pursue your chosen funding model(s). Now it's time to revisit that list and make it much more specific. Maybe you'll need to determine how many more hours of programming each service recipient will need, which personnel will shift into new roles and how they'll get the necessary training to transition successfully, the detailed requirements of your new IT system, or the marketing materials you'll need to develop.

You'll also want to revisit your initial take on whether the potential benefits of the investments outweigh the costs. Make extra certain that they do. If not, cross them off your to-do list. Is your current system good enough for funders, or would incremental improvements make the difference between getting and not getting money? (Of course, there are important reasons to invest in IT systems that do not have funding considerations as their primary impetus—including needing better information on program outcomes so you can refine and improve your programs over time.)

There may very well be many changes worth making—more than you could possibly undertake at once. As with the rest of this process, be focused and disciplined in selecting the few changes that will have the highest impact in setting you up for funding success.

During Step 4, Rare recognized that the organization would need to make investments in personnel. Once it decided to move forward, the team researched in greater depth what it would take to develop a high-performing development team that could cultivate public funding successfully. Additional interviews with peers and public funding contacts indicated that the organization would eventually need to fill a small set of specific, specialized roles. Rare also learned that applying for the contracts generally would require some support from program staff as well, and factored that knowledge into its planning and budgeting. Senior Vice President of Strategy and Growth Martha Piper underscored how useful this research was, sharing that, "This analysis helped me really understand the different types of fundraising professionals I needed to hire."

Lay out specific steps and milestones

Once you've decided on the priority investments, you'll be ready to detail a plan for implementing them, complete with specific milestones to target. As you do so, consider the following tactics we've found work well:

- *Break your broad to-dos down into smaller, more actionable steps.* For example, "develop new marketing materials for high-net-worth donors" might become: (1) identify the key characteristics of high-net-worth donors; (2) prepare a list of key messages to highlight; (3) prepare draft materials, based on key messages; and (4) revise draft materials with team feedback.
- *Get as detailed as you need to for the to-dos to truly feel actionable.* For example, you may find that "identifying the key characteristics of high-net-worth donors" is too vague to marshal your team's efforts, and that crystallizing the individual steps (e.g., interviewing potential donors, speaking with colleagues at peer organizations, and researching the typical behavior of high-net-worth donors) is a better level of detail for your workplan.

- *Assign clear accountability.* Each broad to-do should have an overall point person, and each sub-step should belong to a specific staff member (who may or may not be the same as the overall point person). Set deadlines against each to-do so you can clearly understand if you're on track.
- *Set milestones that focus on results rather than pure process.* Doing so will help you track whether progress on your to-dos is translating to progress on implementing your chosen funding model. A well-developed set of milestones is one that leads, in logical steps, to the ambitious goals you have set. For marketing materials, these might read "By six months, distribute marketing materials to 12 high-net-worth individuals. By 12 months, secure donations from at least three of those individuals."
- *Keep in mind any other major initiatives within your organization that will draw on your team's time and energy.* Make sure your plan is realistic in that context. If it's too much, too fast, adjust your timeline, sequence your initiatives, or otherwise scale back your ambitions.

Communicate, communicate, communicate!

Even the best laid implementation plan will go nowhere if the individuals required to make it happen are not on board. That means committing deeply to communicating at every step of the way. At any given time, are your key stakeholders clear on the plan? Are they aware of the priority investments required to bring the plan to fruition? Are they clear on their roles in making that happen? And are they aware of the progress that has been made and of the roadblocks encountered? Consider these questions periodically, and double-down your communication activities if you come up with "no" or "I'm not sure" answers.

There are a lot of stakeholders to keep in mind here—your senior team, your development team, your staff in general, your board, your key funders. Be thoughtful about the information needs of each (frequency, level of detail, format) and tailor your communications accordingly. For example, perhaps the full development team will need weekly live check-ins, and the board will require monthly memos and quarterly advisory discussions.

Prepare to learn and adjust

The more explicit you are about what you hope to learn as you try to implement your chosen funding model(s), the more likely you are to learn it—and to learn it quickly. This is where setting a formal learning agenda can be invaluable. What key assumptions did you make when you decided to implement a given funding model? How will you understand whether those assumptions were correct or not? Having a learning agenda will make it far easier to see if the beliefs on which you based your choice of funding model are bearing out.

The Rare team, for example, flagged some important areas of uncertainty related to the intricate workings of public funding. It charted a path to clarify them over time, with the development staff lining up discussions with funders, development consultants, and counterparts at peer organizations—so it could ask more specific questions about the rules of public funding and opportunities. Having a clear learning agenda helped the Rare team gather the information it needed to fine-tune the government funding strategy in accordance with the most promising opportunities.

Like Rare, you'll want to keep your eyes wide open to indicators that course corrections are necessary. If you find that you're not hitting multiple milestones and you're debunking key assumptions underlying your choice of funding model, it may be time for you to re-evaluate your approach. This is not unusual. As you move forward in implementation, you're bound to learn more about both internal and external factors that will influence your approach. The most successful organizations are those that are willing to use those real-time learnings to reshape and re-focus their efforts when appropriate. Of course, you don't want to change course drastically at every little setback, but missed milestones should urge careful reflection on what you can do to improve.

See page 52 of **Appendix B** for a summary of Rare's funding strategy implementation plan.

In review: Key questions to consider when developing an implementation plan

- Are key stakeholders—including our board and current staff—on board with the plan?
- Of the many potential changes and investments we could make to increase our success, which will have the most impact for the least cost?
- How will we make sure that our organization is successfully implementing our chosen funding model(s)? How will we hold both individual staff and the organization overall accountable for this success?
- Do we have a clear learning agenda that will help keep us on track?
- Are we making appropriate progress towards our ultimate goal? If not, how can we recalibrate so that we meet the goals we set out for ourselves at the start of this process?

Closing thoughts

We hope this guide helps your organization identify and develop a funding model that supports your aspirations for making a positive difference in the world. What we have described is a journey—probably not a short one, and not necessarily an entirely easy or comfortable one either. In fact, it's unlikely that your organization, as it stands today, is the same organization you'll need to pursue your chosen funding model.

The funding paths that nonprofits take will vary. Some will find models that support large-scale programs, while others will not. All can benefit, however, from greater clarity about how they can sustainably fund their critically important contributions to society.

We believe that a strong funding model provides the essential foundation for programmatic success, while the lack of an intentional funding model can undermine the success of even the most brilliant program model. It's all about investing in your organization's funding strategy with the same intentionality as you invest in its program strategy.

As a result of its search and its effective implementation of a funding model, BELL can now predictably cover 70 percent of its costs in any locality. With this model in place, BELL has been able to expand much more rapidly than originally envisioned. In 2004, when its funding model first took shape, BELL was reaching 1,500 students. Today, it is reaching 15,000.

Rare, while not quite as far along in the journey, is allocating staff time and making key investments to fortify its individual donor-based funding model and to develop a new funding model rooted in government funding. Along the way, the organization is building essential knowledge and experience about how these funding models will work in practice.

With individual funding, Rare has succeeded in spreading fundraising efforts beyond President and CEO Brett Jenks by hiring three additional individual fundraisers. Each covers a specific region of the United States where individuals who support international conservation are clustered, and each has a team of existing major donors and board members providing support.

Rare has also made progress in pursuing public funding. For example, it recently won a $2-million contract from the German development group Deutsche Gesellschaft für Internationale Zusammenarbeit (GIZ) GmbH and is working with US-based government contractor Chemonics on a USAID project. Through its implementation efforts, Rare has learned a lot, and the management team is adapting its plans accordingly. Most notably, the organization has shifted its public funding focus to cultivate the sources that showed the most promise during the first 12 months of piloting the Public Provider model.

There have also been important investments in communications. As Rare has expanded its fundraising staff and programs, its management team has found that it has needed to get really clear on its messaging, so staff can represent the organization's efforts in a consistent way. To that end, Rare is in the middle of a rebranding project.

Reflecting on this journey, Jenks noted, "Clarity is king when running a nonprofit. Picking a sensible revenue model was one of the most liberating and clarifying things we've done to date. I empathize with leaders who constantly wonder (or are constantly asked), why not membership, what about online giving, how about government grants, or fee for service? Taking 'maybe' out of the process has already boosted our bottom line."

Acknowledgements

The thoughtful contributions of numerous individuals and organizations have made the creation of this guide possible. To begin, we truly are indebted to Rare for allowing us to profile its journey in depth. Many thanks go to BELL, the Council of Chief State School Officers, HopeLab, and the other nonprofits whose stories we referenced. We are also grateful for the input we received from Kevin Greer of New Profit, Inc., Martha Piper of Rare, William Stone of ACCESS, and Phillip Vlahakis of Computers for Youth. This guide also reflects the efforts of a team of contributors at Bridgespan including Gihani Fernando, Joe Ferrer, Jacqueline Hadley, Laura Lanzerotti, Carole Matthews, Katie Smith Milway, Alicia Rodriguez, Jen Sauvé, Bradley Seeman, Nan Stone, and Sadie Talmadge. We are particularly grateful to Jenny Jordan and Laura Noonan, who collaborated extensively with us on research and early drafts.

Appendix A:

Sample workplan

	Timing (weeks)	Staff support required (in addition to project lead)	Steering committee role
1	2	• ED • Development team • Finance team	• **Understand** current funding approach
2	3–4	• Junior staff (secondary research and Excel support) • Development team (advisory role)	• **Review** peer research findings (optional meeting)
3	2	• ED • Director of Development • Junior staff who worked on Step 2	• **Approve** subset of funding models to evaluate further
4	3–4	• Junior staff (secondary research) • Development team (advisory role) • Finance team (advisory role)	• **Review** research (can be combined with Step 5 meeting)
5	2	• ED • Director of Development • Senior leadership (programs, operations)	• **Approve** 1–2 funding models to pilot
6	3–4	• Development team • Finance team • Program staff (if program changes required)	• **Approve** implementation and investment plan

Appendix B:

Sample outputs from Step 1
(Analyze your current approach to funding)

Sample Excel spreadsheet

Funding Source	Sub-category	Specific source	Year 1	Year 2	Year 3	Year 4	Year 5	Total (1-5)
Individual	Major gift	Alan Anderson	250,000	250,000	250,000	500,000	500,000	1,750,000
Individual	Major gift	Brian Blocker	500,000	–	–	–	–	500,000
Individual	Small gift	Caroline Callahan	500	500	500	500	500	2,500
Individual	Small gift	Don Devine	25	50	50	100	250	475
Individual	Small gift	Emma Eng	50	–	–	100	100	250
Foundation	National	Big Foundation A	–	300,000	300,000	300,000	–	900,000
Foundation	Community	Community Foundation B	50,000	50,000	50,000	50,000	50,000	250,000
Corporation	Corporate giving	Local Company A	–	–	10,000	10,000	10,000	30,000
Corporation	Sponsorship	Local Company A	10,000	–	–	–	15,000	25,000
Government	National	Federal TRIO Program	75,000	75,000	75,000	75,000	75,000	375,000
Government	State	NJ DOE	50,000	50,000	50,000	50,000	50,000	250,000
Government	Local	Newark Source A	150,000	150,000	150,000	100,000	100,000	650,000
Government	Local	Newark Source B	–	–	250,000	200,000	200,000	650,000
Earned Income	Licensing	Proprietary web-based tool	10,000	10,000	10,000	10,000	10,000	50,000
Total			1,095,575	885,550	1,145,550	1,295,700	1,010,850	5,433,225

Totals by funding source

			Year 1	Year 2	Year 3	Year 4	Year 5	Total (1-5)
Individual			750,575	250,550	250,550	500,700	500,850	2,253,225
Foundation			50,000	350,000	350,000	350,000	50,000	1,150,000
Corporation			10,000	–	10,000	10,000	25,000	55,000
Government			275,000	275,000	525,000	425,000	425,000	1,925,000
Earned Income			10,000	10,000	10,000	10,000	10,000	50,000
Total			1,095,575	885,550	1,145,550	1,295,700	1,010,850	5,433,225

Sample Excel output

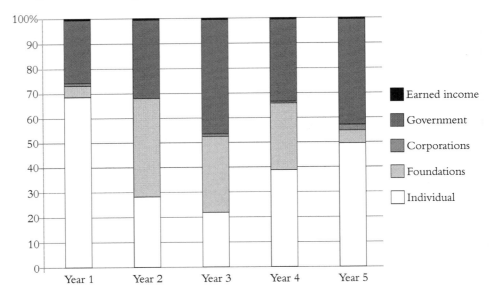

Sample outputs from Step 2 (Learn from the funding approaches of peer organizations)

Sample outputs from peer research

Organization XXX total revenues, in $millions

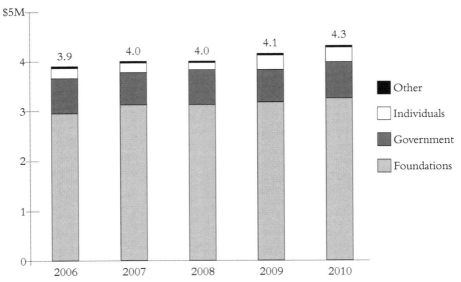

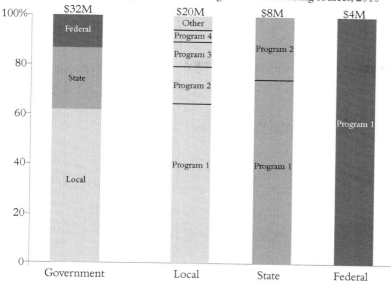

Concentration of organization XXX's government funding sources, 2010

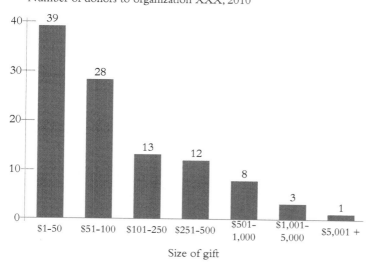

Number of donors to organization XXX, 2010

Sample outputs from Step 6 (Develop an implementation plan)

Rare's public funding model plan and milestones

Public funding strategy overview

Key steps			
Year 1	**Year 2**	**Year 3**	**Year 4**

• Select 3-4 target countries based on:
  - Program alignment
  - Size of funding pool
  - Strength of (or potential for) relationships with stakeholders
	• Select 2-3 additional countries for public funding focus	• Hire two dedicated professionals with public funding experience
		  - Budgeter
		  - Project manager
			• Revisit DC strategy
			  - Consider hiring DC-focused resourc(e.g., lobbyist)
			  - Decision would b« driven by Rare's prc ress on public fundi

• Focus on deepening relationships in target countries
  - Build connections with stakeholders
  - Hire government relationship manager
	• Focus on highlighting progress on current projects with target country missions	• Expand focus to other public funding opportunities
		  - During the first 2 years, pursue other promising sources opportunistically, as needed	

• Use existing staff and consultants to research and pursue public funding opportunities	• Hire two dedicated professionals with public funding familiarity
	  - Proposal writer
	  - Technical advisor
		• Continue to network with peer organizations	

• Invest in developing impact scorecard for public funders	• Increase focus on networking with public funding contacts and other conservation NGOs to stay abreast of conservation policy trends		

Public funding strategy milestones

Milestone	FY10	FY11	FY12	FY13+
Determine short list of public funding priority countries	✓			
Schedule introductory conversations with stakeholders in potential priority countries	✓			
Establish 3-4 priority countries	✓			
Hire relationship manager	✓			
Commit additional investment into impact assessment	✓	✓		
Cultivate relationships with other missions and public funding sources		✓		
Identify additional priority countries		✓		
Commit to regular presence with peer organizations on funding trends		✓		
Hire proposal writer		✓		
Hire technical advisor		✓		
Hire budgeter			✓	
Hire project manager			✓	
Revisit need for DC lobbyist				✓

Appendix C:
How to research funding sources

In addition to asking your board, staff, local experts, funders, and peers for recent information specific to your domain, some general approaches for researching funding sources exist.

Foundation funding

It's unlikely that any one foundation will be a perfect fit for your organization. Instead of looking for that "silver bullet," identify those foundations that seem most aligned with your strengths and start building relationships from there. The most useful information may come from the peer research discussed in Step 2. Look at the websites of organizations like your own or organizations that you aspire to be like. Though you may find lists of funders on the websites of peer organizations, you are unlikely to find actual dollar amounts there. These can be found (sometimes) on the funder's website, and (always) on its Form 990, available through the Foundation Center (www.foundationcenter.org) or Guidestar (www.guidestar.org).

Foundation Center's *Foundation Directory Online* database is a great resource for researching potential foundation funders. This database requires a subscription, but several options are available at reasonable rates. (See the sidebar, "How to use Foundation Center's *Foundation Directory Online* database," on page 54.) The database can provide you with two very important pieces of information. First, it can give you a sense of the overall foundation funding available in your area, which can help you to develop realistic goals for how much your organization could raise. Secondly, it can help you pinpoint the foundations that may be the most likely funders for your organization.

Once you've identified likely foundation funders, you'll need to assess your organization's fit with their missions. Here, diving into foundation websites directly to determine any common characteristics of their grantees may make sense. For example, some foundations may say that grantees from a fairly wide geographical range are eligible, but by examining the list of agencies actually funded, you will get a clearer sense of the geographical areas in which they are most interested. *Getting specific about the criteria they use to evaluate grantees is crucial, since foundations that on the surface look similar may in fact have very different priorities.*

Take the experience of BELL, the youth development organization cited throughout this guide. While working to identify potential new foundation supporters, the organization developed a list of foundations that had historically supported youth development efforts. Further research revealed, however, that less than a quarter of those foundations focused on efforts like BELL's. The foundations that focused on early childhood advocacy, for example, were out. But those that focused on direct service provision of out-of-school time experiences were squarely in.

How to use Foundation Center's *Foundation Directory Online* database

1. From the *Foundation Directory Online* home page, click on the "Search Grants" section. There you will be able to determine total annual giving to the issues and geographies your organization addresses.

2. Once in the "Search Grants" section, you can restrict your search for grants by the categories most relevant to your organization. These include geography (from broad countries to narrow zip codes), recipient type, subject (i.e., issue area), types of support (e.g., building/renovation, program evaluation), and keywords. Note that you may want to do a few searches with different combinations of categories and keywords since some areas are more narrowly defined than others. For example, a search for "crime, public policy" yields about half as many grants as a search for "crime, reform."

3. Also in the "Search Grants" section, you can filter results by grant year and grant amount.

4. Once you have a list of grants, you can export the data to Excel for easier manipulation.

5. Also on Foundation Center, you can research specific funders. If one funder seems particularly promising, navigate to the "Search Grantmakers" tab to learn more about them. There, you can view historical giving patterns, purpose and activities, primary fields of interests, and application information.

Digging deeper into the out-of-school-time foundations, BELL found that some placed a premium on evidence of impact and depth of experience, while others preferred to fund newer, less proven innovations. With its proven programming, BELL was a better fit with foundations in the former camp. Those were the foundations BELL ended up targeting.

In addition to looking at the criteria foundations use to assess grantees, you should also consider the requirements that they place on their grantees. Make sure that the costs to meet those requirements do not trump the value of the grant.

With foundation research, as with hunting for jobs or spouses, actually talking to people trumps Internet research. Find opportunities to meet key staff from foundations you have targeted. Advocacy forums, "meet the funders" events, ribbon-cuttings, and a variety of other local and regional events offer opportunities for funders and nonprofit leaders to meet. Or ask someone to make an introduction, or just send a note.

Government funding

Federal, state, and local government funding sources will all require a different research approach. In all cases, though, interviews with government officials will be essential to truly understand the relevant eligibility rules and process requirements. The political climate is also an ever-present consideration. Are government priorities shifting in a way that would affect the funding stream you're researching? Has that stream lost its key "champion"? Will economic considerations lead to an increase or decrease in dollars? These are all questions organizations should bear in mind when considering a government funding source.

The good news about researching government sources is that, for the most part, all information must be public. The bad news? Much of this information can be difficult to access or understand. Setting up phone calls with the appropriate officials early and often will be key to your ability to answer your most important questions. To identify those officials, do a Google search of the specific funding source. If this approach fails, reach out to the government agency overseeing the funds (e.g., the Department of Education for Title I money) for help in identifying the right person. Also consider how you can tap board members, colleagues at peer organizations, and other contacts to facilitate introductions to and conversations with government decision makers. Though it may require some persistence to schedule a meeting, the benefits of those direct conversations can be huge.

BELL found that one-on-one conversations with government officials were essential. BELL needed to understand if a particular government funding source would require the organization to provide transportation to its students (something BELL did not currently do). An in-depth online search yielded no clear answer, so BELL reached out to the appropriate federal administrator. When that person did not respond right away, BELL leveraged its relationships with donors, intermediaries, and board members. Through that process, BELL was able to get the clear answer it needed: transportation would be required in most cases, so the source might not be a good fit for the organization.

As with foundations, getting a sense of past funding patterns is critical for understanding which government agencies are providing funding, and who and what they are funding. For federal grants, some agencies make it easy to find this information. For example, the Substance Abuse and Mental Health

Services Administration, which oversees much of the government's substance abuse and mental health funding and some of its homelessness and HIV funding, lists grantees by year and program category; within its state-by-state reports, it provides brief summaries of each funded project. The Centers for Disease Control and Prevention, on the other hand, which is by far the largest source of disease prevention funding, often makes it hard (or impossible) to figure out who and what it has funded. One place to look for grantee listings is in an agency's news releases, which often include announcements of funding awards and can usually be easily located on agency websites.

Grants.gov (www.grants.gov) is a great source for real-time information on currently available funding and for funding that has previously been available. It provides links to current and past funding announcements, which contain extensive detail on program requirements, including eligibility. As with foundations, a gap may exist between the kinds of organizations that are theoretically eligible for funding and those that actually get funded. The National Institutes of Health, for example, almost always lists a broad range of eligible entities in its funding announcement, but in practice directs the great bulk of awards to academic institutions.

Subsidy Scope (www.subsidyscope.org), an initiative of the Pew Charitable Trusts, is another helpful website. It allows you to identify specific organizations that are receiving different types of government grants.

For state-level sources, consider starting with the home page of the state department with responsibility for your particular issue area (e.g., the Department of Education for an education nonprofit, the Department of Justice for a juvenile crime organization). Many of these state department home pages will provide links to specific state funding sources. It may take a bit of digging!

Finally, for local grants, the best approach is generally to go straight to the source, whether it be the mayor's office, the school district, the county services' office, or some other local body. Online information may be scarce for local streams, so conversations with key government staff will be particularly important.

Other private giving

Though finding information on other forms of giving (such as corporate and individual) is often harder, there are some sources that may enable you to come up with rough estimates of annual donations in your issue area. The Center on Philanthropy at Indiana University produces *Giving USA*, an annual report on philanthropy (including individual giving) that breaks out donations by domain (e.g., human services, education). The Center on Philanthropy also has a searchable database of individual donors who have made gifts over $1 million (called their Million Dollar List), which can be a useful tool for determining whether peer organizations have been successful in securing major individual and/or corporate investments. Other academic bodies and think tanks—such as the Center for High Impact Philanthropy at the University of Pennsylvania and the Urban Institute's Center on Nonprofits and Philanthropy—allow users to search their rich compendiums of research. If you are looking for state-specific information, it may be worth a quick Google search to see if there are sources that compile high-level data for your state. For example, Associated Grant Makers in Boston produced a 2005 report on average levels of individual giving in Massachusetts.

Note that researching individual and corporate giving may require more time and result in a less complete answer than you'd find with foundation or government sources. As with much of this process, success will hinge on a willingness to move on when the research is "complete enough."

While outside data can provide essential evidence that significant individual and/or corporate giving exists in your issue area, it says little about your own organization's ability to actually secure those funds. Whether you are competitive depends on a variety of factors, including the strength of your narrative, the skill of your development team, and your ability to speak to individual passions and interests. Your historical success in securing individual and corporate gifts is also an important factor to consider. Our research has shown that growing your individual giving, in particular, is often a slow process. At some point, it may make sense to bring in external specialists—such as fundraising consultants—to advise you on how to increase your likelihood of success.

Stanford SOCIAL
INNOVATION REVIEW

Appendix D:
Ten Nonprofit Funding Models
By William Foster, Peter Kim, Barbara Christiansen
Stanford Social Innovation Review, Spring 2009

Money is a constant topic of conversation among nonprofit leaders: How much do we need? Where can we find it? Why isn't there more of it? In tough economic times, these types of questions become more frequent and pressing. Unfortunately, the answers are not readily available. That's because nonprofit leaders are much more sophisticated about creating programs than they are about funding their organizations, and philanthropists often struggle to understand the impact (and limitations) of their donations.

There are consequences to this financial fuzziness. When nonprofits and funding sources are not well matched, money doesn't flow to the areas where it will do the greatest good. Too often, the result is that promising programs are cut, curtailed, or never launched. And when dollars become tight, a chaotic fundraising scramble is all the more likely to ensue.[1]

In the for-profit world, by contrast, there is a much higher degree of clarity on financial issues. This is particularly true when it comes to understanding how different businesses operate, which can be encapsulated in a set of principles known as business models. Although there is no definitive list of corporate business models,[2] there is enough agreement about what they mean that investors and executives alike can engage in sophisticated conversations about any given company's strategy. When a person says that a company is a "low-cost provider" or a "fast follower," the main outlines of how that company operates

[1] In a November 2008 Bridgespan survey of more than 1001 nonprofits, leaders were asked which of eight different and often conflicting fundraising tactics would play some role or a major role in their approach to addressing the downturn. Nearly half (48 percent) of respondents said that six or more would.

[2] For example, see Thomas Malone, Peter Weill, Richard Lai, et al., "Do Some Business Models Perform Better Than Others?" *MIT Sloan Research Paper No. 4615-06*, May 2006.

are pretty clear. Similarly, stating that a company is using "the razor and the razor blade" model describes a type of ongoing customer relationship that applies far beyond shaving products.

The value of such shorthand is that it allows business leaders to articulate quickly and clearly how they will succeed in the marketplace, and it allows investors to quiz executives more easily about how they intend to make money. This back-and-forth increases the odds that businesses will succeed, investors will make money, and everyone will learn more from their experiences.

The nonprofit world rarely engages in equally clear and succinct conversations about an organization's long-term funding strategy. That is because the different types of funding that fuel nonprofits have never been clearly defined.[3] More than a poverty of language, this represents—and results in—a poverty of understanding and clear thinking.

Through our research, we have identified 10 nonprofit models that are commonly used by the largest nonprofits in the United States. Our intent is not to prescribe a single approach for a given nonprofit to pursue. Instead, we hope to help nonprofit leaders articulate more clearly the models that they believe could support the growth of their organizations, and use that insight to examine the potential and constraints associated with those models.

Beneficiaries are not customers

One reason why the nonprofit sector has not developed its own lexicon of funding models is that running a nonprofit is generally more complicated than running a comparable size for-profit business. When a for-profit business finds a way to create value for a customer, it has generally found its source of revenue; the customer pays for the value. With rare exceptions, that is not true in the nonprofit sector. When a nonprofit finds a way to create value for a beneficiary (for example, integrating a prisoner back into society or saving an endangered species), it has not identified its economic engine. That is a separate step.

Duke University business professor J. Gregory Dees, in his work on social entrepreneurship, describes the need to understand both the donor value proposition and the recipient value proposition. Clara Miller, CEO of the Nonprofit Finance Fund, who has also written wonderfully about this dilemma, talks about all nonprofits being in two "businesses"—one related to their program activities and the other related to raising charitable "subsidies."

As a result of this distinction between beneficiary and funder, the critical

---

3 For an early framework looking at "donative" vs. "commercial" nonprofits, see Henry Hansmann, "The Role of Nonprofit Enterprise," *Yale Law Journal*, 89, 5, April 1980.

aspects (and accompanying vocabulary) of nonprofit funding models need to be understood separately from those of the for-profit world. It is also why we use the term *funding model* rather than *business model* to describe the framework. A business model incorporates choices about the cost structure and value proposition to the beneficiary. A funding model, however, focuses only on the funding, not on the programs and services offered to the beneficiary.

All nonprofit executives can use our 10 funding models to improve their fundraising and management, but the usefulness of these models becomes particularly important as nonprofits get bigger. There are many ways to raise as much as $1 million a year, some of which can be improvised during the process. Once organizations try to raise $25 million to $50 million or more each year, however, there are fewer possible paths. The number of potential decision makers who can authorize spending such large amounts of money decreases (or you need to get them en masse), and the factors that motivate these decision makers to say "yes" are more established (or cannot be as thoroughly influenced by one charismatic nonprofit leader).

Our research of large nonprofits confirms this. In a recent study, we identified 144 nonprofit organizations—created since 1970—that had grown to $50 million a year or more in size.[4] We found that each of these organizations grew large by pursuing specific sources of funding—often concentrated in one particular source of funds—that were a good match to support their particular types of work. Each had also built up highly professional internal fundraising capabilities targeted at those sources. In other words, each of the largest nonprofits had a well-developed funding model.

The larger the amount of funding needed, the more important it is to follow preexisting funding markets where there are particular decision makers with established motivations. Large groups of individual donors, for example, are already joined by common concerns about various issues, such as breast cancer research. And major government funding pools, to cite another example, already have specific objectives, such as foster care. Although a nonprofit that needs a few million dollars annually may convince a handful of foundations or wealthy individuals to support an issue that they had not previously prioritized, a nonprofit trying to raise tens of millions of dollars per year can rarely do so.

This is not to say that funding markets are static; they aren't. The first Earth Day in 1970 coincided with a major expansion in giving to environmental causes; the Ethiopian famine of 1984-85 led to a dramatic increase in support for international relief; and awareness of the U.S. educational crisis in the late

4 William Foster and Gail Fine, "How Nonprofits Get Really Big," *Stanford Social Innovation Review*

1980s laid the groundwork for charter school funding. Changes cannot be foreseen, however, and, hence, can not be depended on as a source of funding. In addition, these changes were the product or culmination of complex national and international events, not the result of a single nonprofit's work.

Earl Martin Phalen, cofounder of BELL, an after-school and summer educational organization, captured the benefits of such intentionality well, summing up his experience for a group of nonprofit leaders in 2007. "Our fundraising strategy used to be 'let's raise more money this year than last' and we always were unsure of where we'd be. Then we got serious in thinking about our model and identified an ongoing type of government funding that was a good match for our work. While it required some program changes to work, we now predictably cover 70 percent of our costs in any locality through this approach."

Ten funding models

Devising a framework for nonprofit funding presents challenges. To be useful, the models cannot be too general or too specific. For example, a community health clinic serving patients covered by Medicaid and a nonprofit doing development work supported by the U.S. Agency for International Development are both government funded, yet the type of funding they get, and the decision makers controlling the funding, are very different. Lumping the two together in the same model would not be useful. At the same time, designating a separate model for nonprofits that receive Title I SES funds, for example, is too narrow to be useful.

In the end, we settled on three parameters to define our funding models—the source of funds, the types of decision makers, and the motivations of the decision

Identifying the Models

We started by identifying a pool of nonprofits to study by combining *The NonProfit Times'* "Top 100" list (from 2006) with our list of 144 nonprofits founded since 1970 that have reached $50-million or greater in size. Several major types of nonprofits (for example, hospitals, universities, and religious congregations) were not represented in this sample so we added them to our pool. Next, we collected revenue and funding data for each sample organization. As we categorized the data, we began to identify funding patterns. Each major funding source (for example, government) broke into a handful of sub-sources that represented distinct decision makers and motivations and linked remarkably well to the organization's missions and domains. At the end of this process, we had 10 funding models. Then, we interviewed the leaders of organizations that epitomize each model. Our goal in the interviews was to explore the challenges and trade-offs of each model, and to better understand the drivers of successful fundraising within each model.

makers. This allowed us to identify 10 distinct funding models at level that is broadly relevant yet defines real choices.

It is interesting to note that there were several funding models we thought we might find, but didn't. One possible model was nonprofits supported by earned-income ventures distinct and separate from their core mission-related activities. Another possible model was nonprofits that operated on a strictly fee-for-service model in either a business-to-business or direct-to-consumer fashion, without important supplementary fundraising (from members or prior beneficiaries) or underlying government support. Although there are some nonprofits supporting themselves with such funding approaches, they were not present among the large nonprofits that we studied. It is our belief that these types of approaches do not lend themselves to large-scale, sustained nonprofit advantage over for-profit entities.

What follows are descriptions of the 10 funding models, along with profiles of representative nonprofits for each model. The models are ordered by the dominant type of funder. The first three models (Heartfelt Connector, Beneficiary Builder, and Member Motivator) are funded largely by many individual donations. The next model (Big Bettor) is funded largely by a single person or by a few individuals or foundations. The next three models (Public Provider, Policy Innovator, and Beneficiary Broker) are funded largely by the government. The next model (Resource Recycler) is supported largely by corporate funding. And the last two models (Market Maker and Local Nationalizer) have a mix of funders.

1. **Heartfelt Connector**: Some nonprofits, such as the Make-a-Wish Foundation, grow large by focusing on causes that resonate with the existing concerns of large numbers of people at all income levels, and by creating a structured way for these people to connect where none had previously existed. Nonprofits that take this approach use a funding model we call the *Heartfelt Connector*. Some of the more popular causes are in the environmental, international, and medical research areas. They are different from nonprofits that tap individuals with particular religious beliefs, political leanings, or sporting interests, who come together to form organizations in the course of expressing their interests. Heartfelt Connectors often try to build explicit connections between volunteers through special fundraising events.

   The Susan G. Komen Foundation is an example of a nonprofit that uses the Heartfelt Connector model. Established in 1982, the Komen Foundation works through a network of 125 affiliates to eradicate breast cancer as a life-threatening disease by funding research grants, by supporting education, screening, and treatment projects in communities around the world, and by educating women about the importance of early detection. The foundation's mission has a deep resonance with many women, even though its work may never benefit them directly. Between 1997 and 2007 the Komen Foundation's annual fundraising grew from $47 million to $334 million. The average individual donation is small, about $33, but the foundation's fundraising efforts have been driven by its ability to reach out to an ever-widening base of support. Its major fundraising vehicle is the Susan G. Komen Race for the Cure. The foundation and its affiliates hold about 120 running races each year that draw more than 1 million participants. These events not only allow individuals to give money; they also engage volunteers to put together teams, solicit funds, and participate in the race day experience.

Nonprofit leaders considering the Heartfelt Connector funding model should ask themselves the following questions:
- Have a large cross section of people already shown that they will fund causes in this domain?
- Can we communicate what is compelling about our nonprofit in a simple and concise way?
- Does a natural avenue exist to attract and involve large numbers of volunteers?
- Do we have, or can we develop, the in-house capabilities to attempt broad outreach in even one geographic area?

2. **Beneficiary Builder**: Some nonprofits, such as the Cleveland Clinic, are reimbursed for services that they provide to specific individuals, but rely on people who have benefited in the past from these services for additional donations. We call the funding model that these organizations use the *Beneficiary Builder*. Two of the best examples of Beneficiary Builders are hospitals and universities. Generally, the vast majority of these nonprofits' funding comes from fees that beneficiaries pay for the services the nonprofits provide. But the total cost of delivering the benefit is not covered by the fees. As a result, the nonprofit tries to build long-term relationships with people who have benefited from the service to provide supplemental support, hence the name Beneficiary Builder. Although these donations are often small relative to fees (averaging approximately 5 percent at hospitals and 30 percent at private universities), these funds are critical sources of income for major projects such as building, research, and endowment funds. Donors are often motivated to give money because they believe that the benefit they received changed their life. Organizations using a Beneficiary Builder model tend to obtain the majority of their charitable support from major gifts.

Princeton University is an example of a nonprofit that uses the Beneficiary Builder model. The university has become very adept at tapping alumni for donations, boasting the highest alumni-giving rate among national universities—59.2 percent. In 2008, more than 33,000 undergraduate alumni donated $43.6 million to their alma mater. As a result of the school's fundraising prowess, more than 50 percent of Princeton's operating budget is paid for by donations and earnings from its endowment.

Nonprofit leaders considering the Beneficiary Builder funding model should ask themselves the following questions:

- Does our mission create an individual benefit that is also perceived as an important social good?
- Do individuals develop a deep loyalty to the organization in the course of receiving their individual benefit?
- Do we have the infrastructure to reach out to beneficiaries in a scalable fashion?

3. **Member Motivator:** There are some nonprofits, such as Saddleback Church, that rely on individual donations and use a funding model we call *Member Motivator.* These individuals (who are members of the nonprofit) donate money because the issue is integral to their everyday life and is something from which they draw a collective benefit. Nonprofits using the Member Motivator funding model do not create the rationale for group activity, but instead connect with members (and donors) by offering or supporting the activities that they already seek. These organizations are often involved in religion, the environment, or arts, culture, and humanities.

The National Wild Turkey Federation (NWTF), which protects and expands wild turkey habitats and promotes wild turkey hunting, is an example of a Member Motivator. It attracts turkey hunters, who collectively benefit from NWTF's work and therefore become loyal members and fundraisers. Local NWTF members host more than 2,000 fundraising banquets each year, raising about 80 percent of the organization's annual revenues. These banquets provide multiple donation opportunities: entry tickets (which cost about $50 each and include an annual membership); merchandise purchase (averaging more than $100 per attendee); and raffle tickets (generating about $16,000 per banquet). NWTF's national headquarters supplies raffle prizes and merchandise to sell at these banquets. Each banquet clears an average of $10,000 after expenses. A significant portion of the money raised is dedicated to land and turkey conservation in the community from which it was donated.

Nonprofit leaders considering the Member Motivator funding model should ask themselves the following questions:

- Will our members feel that the actions of the organization are directly benefiting them, even if the benefit is shared collectively?
- Do we have the ability to involve and manage our members in fundraising activities?

- Can we commit to staying in tune with, and faithful to, our core membership, even if it means turning down funding opportunities and not pursuing activities that fail to resonate with our members?

4. **Big Bettor**: There are a few nonprofits, such as the Stanley Medical Research Institute, that rely on major grants from a few individuals or foundations to fund their operations. We call their funding model the *Big Bettor*. Often, the primary donor is also a founder, who wants to tackle an issue that is deeply personal to him or her. Although Big Bettors often launch with significant financial backing already secured, allowing them to grow large quickly, there are other instances when an existing organization gets the support of a major donor who decides to fund a new and important approach to solving a problem. The nonprofits we identified as Big Bettors are focused either on medical research or on environmental issues. The primary reasons that Big Bettors can attract sizable donations are: the problem being addressed can potentially be solved with a huge influx of money (for example, a vast sum can launch a research institute to cure a specific illness); or the organization is using a unique and compelling approach to solve the problem.

   Conservation International (CI), whose mission is to conserve the Earth's biodiversity and to demonstrate that humans can live harmoniously with nature, is an example of a nonprofit that uses the Big Bettor funding model. CI's ability to identify locations around the world where protecting an area of land can have a significant effect on preserving global biodiversity helps it attract donors who are willing to contribute large amounts of money so that they can have an important and lasting impact on protecting the Earth. The majority of CI's contributions come from a few large donors.

   Nonprofit leaders considering the Big Bettor funding model should ask themselves the following questions:
   - Can we create a tangible and lasting solution to a major problem in a foreseeable time frame?
   - Can we clearly articulate how we will use large-scale funding to achieve our goals?
   - Are any of the wealthiest individuals or foundations interested in our issue and approach?

5. **Public Provider**: Many nonprofits, such as the Success for All Foundation, work with government agencies to provide essential social services, such as housing, human services, and education, for which the government has previously defined and allocated funding. Nonprofits that provide these services use a funding model we call *Public Provider*. In some cases, the government outsources the service delivery function but establishes specific

requirements for nonprofits to receive funding, such as reimbursement formulae or a request for proposal (RFP) process. As Public Providers grow, they often seek other funding sources to augment their funding base.

TMC (formerly the Texas Migrant Council), which supports children and families in migrant and immigrant communities, is an example of an organization that uses the Public Provider funding model. At its inception in 1971, TMC tapped into the federal government's Head Start program to fund its initial work, helping children prepare for school by focusing on the bilingual and bicultural needs of families. As TMC grew, its leaders sought to reduce its dependence on this one funding source and to identify other government funds. TMC now receives funding from a variety of federal, state, and local government sources. TMC has expanded from Texas into seven additional states and is offering new programs, such as literacy, prenatal care, and consumer education.

Nonprofit leaders considering the Public Provider funding model should ask themselves the following questions:
- Is our organization a natural match with one or more large, preexisting government programs?
- Can we demonstrate that our organization will do a better job than our competitors?
- Are we willing to take the time to secure contract renewals on a regular basis?

6. **Policy Innovator**: Some nonprofits, such as Youth Villages, rely on government money and use a funding model we call *Policy Innovator*. These nonprofits have developed novel methods to address social issues that are not clearly compatible with existing government funding programs. They have convinced government funders to support these alternate methods, usually by presenting their solutions as more effective and less expensive than existing programs. (By contrast, Public Providers tap into existing government programs to provide funds for the services they offer.)

An example of a Policy Innovator is HELP USA. This nonprofit provides transitional housing for the homeless and develops affordable permanent housing for low-income families. Andrew Cuomo (son of former New York governor Mario Cuomo) founded HELP USA in 1986 as an alternative to New York's approach of paying hotels to house the homeless in so-called "welfare hotels." HELP USA's innovative approach to the housing crisis came about in an era when homelessness was a prominent public issue and government funders were willing to try a novel approach. Cuomo gained the initial support of government decision makers by positioning his solution as both more effective and less costly, which was critical during New York's fiscal crisis. In 2007, HELP

USA's revenues were $60 million, almost 80 percent of which came from government sources, half federal and half state and local. The organization was operating in New York City, Philadelphia, Las Vegas, Houston, and Buffalo, N.Y.

Nonprofit leaders considering the Policy Innovator funding model should ask themselves the following questions:
- Do we provide an innovative approach that surpasses the status quo (in impact and cost) and is compelling enough to attract government funders, which tend to gravitate toward traditional solutions?
- Can we provide government funders with evidence that our program works?
- Are we willing and able to cultivate strong relationships with government decision makers who will advocate change?
- At this time are there sufficient pressures on government to overturn the status quo?

7. **Beneficiary Broker**: Some nonprofits, such as the Iowa Student Loan Liquidity Corporation, compete with one another to provide government-funded or backed services to beneficiaries. Nonprofits that do this use what we call a *Beneficiary Broker* funding model. Among the areas where Beneficiary Brokers compete are housing, employment services, health care, and student loans. What distinguishes these nonprofits from other government-funded programs is that the beneficiaries are free to choose the nonprofit from which they will get the service.

The Metropolitan Boston Housing Partnership (MBHP), a regional nonprofit administering state and federal rental assistance voucher programs in 30 Massachusetts communities, is an example of a nonprofit that uses the Beneficiary Broker funding model. Since launching the organization in 1991, MBHP has developed a reputation as a reliable provider of housing vouchers for families in need. MBHP is the largest provider of housing vouchers in the Boston area, connecting more than 7,500 families to housing at any one time. MBHP also provides related services, such as education and homelessness prevention programs. More than 90 percent of MBHP's revenue comes from the small administrative fees the state provides as part of the voucher program. The remaining funds come from corporations and foundations.

Nonprofit leaders considering the Beneficiary Broker funding model should ask themselves the following questions:
- Can we demonstrate to the government our superior ability to connect benefit or voucher holders with benefits, such as successful placement rates and customer satisfaction feedback?
- Can we develop supplemental services that maximize the value of the benefit?

- Can we master the government regulations and requirements needed to be a provider of these benefits?
- Can we find ways to raise money to supplement the fees we receive from the benefits program?

8. **Resource Recycler**: Some nonprofits, such as AmeriCares Foundation, have grown large by collecting in-kind donations from corporations and individuals, and then distributing these donated goods to needy recipients who could not have purchased them on the market. Nonprofits that operate these types of programs use a funding model we call *Resource Recycler*. Businesses are willing to donate goods because they would otherwise go to waste (for example, foods with an expiration date), or because the marginal cost of making the goods is low and they will not be distributed in markets that would compete with the producer (for example, medications in developing countries). In kind donations typically account for the majority of revenues, but Resource Recyclers must raise additional funds to support their operating costs. The vast majority of Resource Recyclers are involved in food, agriculture, medical, and nutrition programs and often are internationally focused.

The Greater Boston Food Bank (TGBFB), the largest hunger relief organization in New England, is an example of a nonprofit that uses the Resource Recycler funding model. This organization distributes nearly 30 million pounds of food annually to more than 600 local organizations, including food pantries, soup kitchens, day care centers, senior centers, and homeless shelters. TGBFB acquires goods in many ways. The dominant sources of goods are retailers and manufacturers. It also receives surplus food from restaurants and hotels. In 2006, corporate in-kind support accounted for 52 percent of TGBFB's revenues. Federal and state government programs provide TGBFB with in-kind goods and money, accounting for 23 percent of its annual budget, which TGBFB uses to purchase food for distribution. Cash donations from individuals make up the remaining 25 percent of revenues, covering overhead and capital improvements.

Nonprofit leaders considering the Resource Recycler funding model should ask themselves the following questions:
- Are the products that we distribute likely to be donated on an ongoing basis?
- Can we develop the expertise to stay abreast of trends in the industries that donate products to us so that we can prepare for fluctuations in donations?
- Do we have a strategy for attracting the cash we'll need to fund operations and overhead?

9. **Market Maker**: Some nonprofits, such as the Trust for Public Land, provide a service that straddles an altruistic donor and a pay or motivated by market forces. Even though there is money available to pay for the service, it would be unseemly or unlawful for a for-profit to do so. Nonprofits that provide these services use a funding model we call *Market Maker*. Organ donation is one example where Market Makers operate. There is a demand for human organs, but it is illegal to sell them. These nonprofits generate the majority of their revenues from fees or donations that are directly linked to their activities. Most Market Makers operate in the area of health and disease, but some also operate in the environmental protection area (for example, land conservation).

The American Kidney Fund (AKF) is an example of a nonprofit that uses the Market Maker funding model. AKF was founded in 1971 to help low-income people with kidney failure pay for dialysis. It is now the country's leading source of financial aid to kidney dialysis patients, providing (in 2006) $82 million in annual grants to 63,500 kidney patients (about 19 percent of all dialysis patients). Before 1996, health care providers were allowed to pay Medicare Part B and Medigap premiums (approximately 20 percent of total costs) for needy dialysis patients. In 1996, the federal government made it illegal for providers to do this because it might trap the patient into receiving dialysis from a particular provider. The new law left thousands of kidney patients unable to afford kidney treatment. AKF noticed this gap and established a program to fill it. AKF now pays these premiums, allowing patients to continue their treatment. AKF is funded primarily by health care providers and other corporations. AKF is now applying the same principles used in its kidney dialysis program for pharmaceuticals used to treat bone loss.

Nonprofit leaders considering the Market Maker funding model should ask themselves the following questions:
- Is there a group of funders with a financial interest in supporting our work?
- Are there legal or ethical reasons why it would be more appropriate for a nonprofit to deliver the services?
- Do we already have a trusted program and brand name?

10. **Local Nationalizer**: There are a number of nonprofits, such as Big Brothers Big Sisters of America, that have grown large by creating a national network of locally based operations. These nonprofits use a funding model we call *Local Nationalizers*. These organizations focus on issues, such as poor schools or children in need of adult role models, that are important to local communities across the country, where government alone can't solve the problem. Most of the money for programs is raised locally, often from individual or corporate donations and special events. Very little of the money comes from government agencies or fees. Very few local operations exceed $5 million in size, but, in totality they can be quite large.

Teach for America (TFA) is an example of a nonprofit that uses a Local Nationalizer funding model. TFA recruits, trains, and places recent college graduates into teaching positions in schools across the country. TFA was founded in 1989, and by 2007 had more than $90 million in annual revenues. The organization relies on its 26 regional TFA offices to raise more than 75 percent of its funding. The reason this works is that TFA's mission—improving the quality of K-12 education—resonates with local funders. TFA developed a culture in which fundraising is considered a critical aspect of the organization at every level, and it recruited local executive directors who would take ownership of attracting regional funding growth.

Nonprofit leaders considering the Local Nationalizer funding model should ask themselves the following questions:
- Does our cause address an issue that local leaders consider a high priority, and is this issue compelling in communities across the country?
- Does expanding our organization into other communities fulfill our mission?
- Can we replicate our model in other communities?
- Are we committed to identifying and empowering high-performing leaders to run local branches of our organization in other communities?

Implications for nonprofits

In the current economic climate it is tempting for nonprofit leaders to seek money wherever they can find it, causing some nonprofits to veer off course. That would be a mistake. During tough times it is more important than ever for nonprofit leaders to examine their funding strategy closely and to be disciplined about the way that they raise money. We hope that this article provides a framework for nonprofit leaders to do just that.

The funding paths that nonprofits take will vary, and not all will find models that support large-scale programs. The good news is that all nonprofits can benefit from greater clarity about their most effective funding model, and it is possible for some nonprofits to develop models that raise large amounts of money. As mentioned earlier, almost 150 new nonprofits (not counting universities and hospitals), surpassed $50 million in annual revenues between 1970 and 2003.

On the other side of the equation, philanthropists are becoming more disciplined about their nonprofit investing. A growing number of foundations, such as the Edna McConnell Clark Foundation and New Profit Inc., are investing in their grantees to improve both program and funding models. We hope that this article helps philanthropists become clearer about their funding strategy so that they can support their programs more effectively.

As society looks to the nonprofit sector and philanthropy to solve important problems, a realistic understanding of funding models is increasingly important to realizing those aspirations.

Made in the USA
Charleston, SC
06 October 2011